1

"extras", changes and terms – some definitions

Extras.

In the dictionaries "extras" has various meanings. We have adopted:

- items which are more than usual, due, expected and,

- items which are subject to additional charges.

Other meanings of "extras" which are not applicable include:

- persons engaged temporarily to fill out crowd scenes in films or plays – as in a recent UK television series,

- special issues of newspapers – as in "Extra. Extra. Read all about it!",

- attractive additions as accessories – as frills or functionalities on cars or mobile phones,

- in cricket: runs scored other than from being hit from the bat, which are credited to the batting side rather than the batsman.

Isn't the English language a wonderful thing?

Changes.

"Changes" also has various meanings.

We have adopted:

- Replacing something with something else, especially something of the same kind that is newer or better.

- Substituting one thing for another.

Other meanings of "changes" which are not applicable include:

- Putting on different clothes.

- Coins as opposed to bank notes.

- An order of a peel of bells.

- What traffic lights do and also gears in cars.

- To obtain a different currency.

- What happens to babies nappies.

- The menopause.

- Moving from one mode of transport to another.

Isn't the English language still a wonderful thing?

Terms.

In these situations, and throughout this volume, the terms "**commission**", "**appointment**" and "**project**" are used specifically and are not generally interchangeable.

In these situations the phrases "**exceeding the norm**" or "**reasonably anticipated**" or similar may arise. These mean considerably exceeding the norm, not just by a few percent or a bit of inconvenience.

"**Further**", "**extra**" and "**additional**" are generally interchangeable.

CHECKLIST – basic steps.

Hello! Let's start sensibly at the beginning with ten basic steps when it comes to extras and extra fees.

Step One: Amongst other things, when involved with opportunities and enquiries with proposals and bids, please identify the extras or changes which are likely to arise during the project and to the services – from checklists and experience, by stages and overall.

Step Two: Check that suitable provisions to deal with such extras and changes are within the orders, contracts or appointment documents – and the provisions are clear, comprehensive, fair and quantifiable – as standard terms and conditions.

Step Three: However if extras and changes are likely or inevitable but costs will be difficult to recover, please make suitable contingency provisions in the base fee or tender. Or provide exclusion clauses or limits and seek agreement. Please make suitable provisions on to the base fee and within the tender – as risk provision or "safety net".

STEP FOUR: Please undertake Steps 1, 2 and 3 **before** entering into or signing any agreement or starting work! Or cap the scope, values or durations of initial or next stage involvements – in writing.

Step Five: When appointed, communicate the arrangements and boundaries concerning extras and changes to key project staff.

Step Six: As the possible extras or changes arise, verify how they are covered within the agreements, and apply the arrangements.

Step Seven: If significant resources and cost will be incurred in assessing or implementing each extra or change, obtain understandings on payments – in detail or in principle – in advance. Or decline. Or dip into the contingency provisions. Or sacrifice some margin / profit.

Step Eight: Identify and regularly maintain the procedures, lines of communication and contacts for addressing and recovering additional costs.

Step Nine: Monitor patterns of extras and changes, with their fee recovery or compensation or impacts on contingency provisions or bottom line.

Step Ten: Please make sure the base services, outputs, products and deliverables are fully, promptly and properly provided, so there are no excuses, set offs or counterclaims that may affect the entitlements arising from the extras and changes.

If these steps are not in place or are not working nicely, please consider the contents and features provided within this practical guide.

Read through, dip in, pick and choose, do exercises, delegate, discuss, use as a reference, etc. Best wishes.

"An indispensable guide for senior management through to students to navigate the choppy waters when seeking additional fees – with immediate payback."

A leading architect.

"I think you have covered the topic comprehensively and the contents are easy to read – so this will appeal to all types of professional. Copies all round!"

An esteemed project manager.

"There's a lot of important and interesting stuff in here. The initial fee negotiation at the outset is crucial. If you anticipate prolongation, for example, you should try to build some "fat" into the fee."

A wise architectural founding partner.

"Really, really useful, well set out, logical order, easy to read."

A respected development advisor.

Everyone at **dashdot publications** wishes to express their thanks and appreciation to our colleagues and contacts for their perceptive and knowledgeable comments and contributions on the journey of assembling this volume. Thank you indeed. The contents remain our responsibility.

extras and changes

– scope, time, people, resources, services... and **fees**

by

Tom Taylor

illustrated by

Ed Rhodes

design and layout by

Rob Dee

a practical guide

the dashdot series

 ◀ **recession survival – a self-assembly kit for businesses of all sizes**

68pp Illustrated
978-0-9574834-4-6

 ◀ **an introduction to the ever expanding design team**

100pp Illustrated
978-0-9574834-0-8

 **sixteen stories** ▶

68pp Illustrated
978-0-9554132-7-8

 ◀ **recession recovery (and beyond) – for businesses of all sizes**

76pp Illustrated
978-0-9574834-5-3

 ◀ **an introduction to and a study guide for collaboration**

GMPM and other afflictions affecting Project Managers ▶

128pp Illustrated
978-0-9574834-1-5

36pp Illustrated
978-0-9554132-2-3

 ◀ **good business advisors – a guide for organisations of all sizes**

48pp Illustrated
978-0-9574834-6-0

 ◀ **how to select the right project manager (under revision)**

time matters ▶

124pp Illustrated
978-0-9554132-3-0

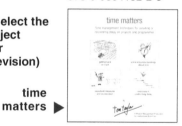

36pp Illustrated
978-0-9574834-3-9

 ◀ **pandemic impacts and responses – for businesses of all sizes (free download)**

32pp Illustrated
978-0-9574834-7-7

 ◀ **leadership in action**

sustainability interventions – for managers of projects and programmes ▶

76pp Illustrated
978-0-9554132-9-2

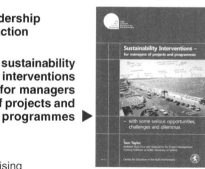

88pp Illustrated
978-0-9554132-8-5

'**Sustainability Interventions**' and the dashdot foundation series, currently comprising '**Meet the Managers**' and '**Management in the Real World**' are available as free downloads. For details and pricing of all dashdot publications please visit: **dashdotpublications.co.uk**

contents

features

To support the texts there are a range of related illustrations, some checklists, a few extra notes, some case studies and appendices to suit.

Hopefully there is something for everyone, in suitable formats to read through, or pick and choose, or probe when needed.

McGivity Conundrums
Nine exercises in Appendix A.

preamble

These notes are to assist architectural and other professional practices with investigating and getting their acts together when it comes to asking for extra fees when they have undertaken extra work, and feel there is an entitlement.

Such practices will include one-person-bands, micro-, mini-, medium- and large-scale practices including mega, international, multi-professional organisations. They all face the dilemmas and difficulties of seeking additional fees for extra work and changes in some way or another and at some time or another.

This material can be adapted to the practice culture or ethos, circumstances or business outlooks on such matters and their terminologies and vocabularies in construction and property sectors.

The prime targets are:

- Director, Partner, Owner, Founder levels – who would like to make better margins for the practice and for themselves – with or without upsetting anyone – too much – and maintaining profession outputs to design standards.

- Practice and studio managers with managerial, financial and administrative responsibilities for the practice to hit its targets and optimise income.

- Associates and senior staff who have mixed practice / studio / team / project involvements plus influence and responsibilities when it comes to extra fees.

- Job runners and project architects and designers who are in the front line and wedded to their projects, teams and clients. They can also see first-hand what is happening on their commissions on such matters; and can apply their experience from previous employments and involvements

- Assistant architects, designers, engineers, managers, surveyors, etc. who can assist, observe and learn about such matters as extra fees; and may require a working knowledge or appreciation to pass their examinations and become fully qualified.

- And working combinations of all the above to address and resolve such matters in theory and in practice.

Common approaches and mutual support within a practice can be most helpful in such matters including within Quality Assurance. These notes with checklists will assist in defining, arranging and applying such approaches and support.

And these original or edited notes can also be used as background reading, or as a paper for delegates to read and then discuss in a workshop format, with case studies and exercises, contributions and typical documentation as provided in this volume.

Good luck with it all – in theory and in practice.

tom taylor

foreword

Extras happen! Extras happen on projects and enterprises. There can be:

- extra scope, activities and changes,

- extra time, durations and prolongations,

- extra and changes to people and participants

- extra resources to get things done,

- extra duties and services above the norm or as originally agreed, all of which with possible entitlements to extra fees and rewards

Asking for additional fees, efficiently and effectively for growing numbers of commissions is going to become really important and absolutely necessary for the survival, prosperity and morale of many conventional and niche architectural and other professional practices – including engineering, surveying and management practices, plus Design and Build organisations .

In multi-project practices there will be a mixed portfolio of commissions with variable "extras". Some commissions will be more profitable than others; some will have more contractual opportunities and technical circumstances to ask for additional fees; and some will have favourable responses and circumstances to receive agreement and payment of extra fees. That's all good!

The reverse will be when commissions are less profitable, not breaking even or making a loss.

There may also be fewer opportunities to apply for extra fees; and even then, the chances of obtaining payment may not be certain. That's not so good – but clear!

Asking for extra costs and fees have become more common in society. Sometimes these additions may be undisclosed by the vendor but still in the "small print" of contract / agreement / order and may be unexpected by the purchaser – until they arise. Thus additional fees can be common and also contentious these days.

For example additional fees for extra or optional services or benefits (as "add-ons") are prevalent in industries such as hotels, airlines, telecoms, computer hardware and software, motor vehicles, health, banking, insurances, white goods, delivery logistics, etc.

Extras may be 'free' or paid for. They may be entirely optional through to essential as in will-not-really-work-without or be fit for required purposes. These extras may be called 'bells and whistles'. They may extend to services charges, gratuities, tips, warranties, legal expenses in insurances, petrol in the tank, out of hours deliveries, etc.

Contractors, subcontractors and suppliers in the construction industry in UK can also appear to be competently and confidently on the case when it comes to their entitlements. However others appear to be a bit slow, less confident and even diffident – notably some of those providing architectural services.

Progressively there are widening understandings or expectations of the likelihood of extra fee income in society, industry and commercial transactions.

One of the causes of these additional charges is the need, when bidding for work, for suppliers and vendors of goods and services to be competitive in their marketplaces. They need to offer attractive packages at attractive prices that beat, match or at least are close to the opposition. There may also be fundamental reductions or restrictions to the base or basic services now involving down-scoping and down-specing to make them affordable for the supplier to supply. Reductions in contingency provisions, profit levels or margins on base services may also be necessary to offer the lowest prices. Modern technology, automation and standardisation are also means of reducing costs and therefore prices.

Generally, the expectations and likelihoods of customers wanting additional services are increasing. The abilities of suppliers to absorb costs of extra provisions or requirements are reducing. And so the necessities to ask for additional fees for extra work are greater – for survival and prosperity, while giving the customers what they need or want. Such changes and pressures are becoming commonplace – and they are increasing.

These scenarios may apply to architectural and other professional practices with their clients as much as any other suppliers with their customers – frequently, increasingly, interestingly.

A CHECKLIST for job runners:

1. Have you read your appointment document for this commission?
2. Have you read the sections on additional fees?
3. Are there agreed charge-out rates for grades of staff?
4. Is there a change control system?
5. Do you know who manages the change control system?
6. Can you charge for change assessments?
7. Can you include change implementation estimates within change assessments?
8. Is there an operational internal timesheet system?
9. Does this timesheet system accommodate "extras" and "changes"?
10. Is it part of your role to identify extra efforts for extra fees?
11. Is it part of your role to liaise with senior persons internally on extra fees?
12. Is it part of your role to inform and liaise with the client externally on extra fees?
13. Do you know the status of extra fees on your project – past, current, future?
14. Anything else?

CASE STUDIES:
The Simple Trap.

We fell into the simple trap!

The commission was just up our street, in the next street and we needed the work and the income. So we quoted a competitive 4% fee plus VAT for architectural services – for a builder / developer enquiry for "up to £20m residential scheme in the town centre". There were no further details or terms or conditions from the client side; and we did not offer any or refer to standard conditions. It all seemed quite simple.

It appeared that the development would be completed in two and half years and be standard units.

- It did not start for a year and then took a further three and half years.

- In the end it was 40% newbuild and 60% conversion of the warehouse – which we had thought would probably be demolished.

- Although there were lots of two-bedroom units there were twenty-five types owing to configurations of cores and service risers affecting bathroom and kitchen layouts. The repetition was limited.

- The external works and landscaping were complex. Sorting out the ponding problems on the paving went on for ages.

- The show flat was a continuing problem with finishes and how to get to it.

- The works were suspended and restarted several times on site – to suit marketing and sales of units.

- Our expenses and disbursements were deemed to be included – because we had not said anything in our proposal. Fortunately travel was minimal.

- The construction final account was £19m. We received 4% plus VAT.

- Thank goodness we quoted "plus VAT" initially!

It is believed that the builder developer made a killing in a seller's market.

Situation: This commission probably held back the practice for several years and we can walk past it every day.

Moral: Nowadays we always, ALWAYS, follow the professional guidelines for our proposals, bidding and agreeing appointments. Never, NEVER, again will we fall into the simple trap.

Observation: Contract law conventions state that a contract exists with offer and acceptance with consideration. It is that simple.

EXTRA NOTES:

Additional Fees in Perspective

Architects and designers charge fees to cover their planned costs or overheads or outgoings with some contingency for the unplanned and to make a profit or surplus or margin.

The overhead usually covers 'fixed' costs of rent, rates, utilities, consumables, admin costs and, significantly, 'unfixed' staff remuneration, principally as salaries – as a base fee.

The contingency is for risk involvements that may occur and have not been reflected in the base fee particularly requiring additional resources and expertise and/or over longer periods. The risks can be few or many, representing the project itself or familiarity with this sector, client, location etc. – and so can be from a low to high percentage and value.

If only sufficient fees are received to cover the overhead, then the organisation is breaking even. If even less is received, then the organisation is operating at a loss.

Most practices would like to make a steady profit target on all commissions. However sometimes some commissions will consume all the base fee and all the contingency and thus reduce or eliminate the target profit.

This may be seen and exacerbated when it is decided to bid and secure work "at cost" / without contingency / without profit. This may be to break into a new market by offering a full service for a discounted fee. Or to maintain turnover and employment of staff. Similarly it may be decided to undertake some pro bono work for a good cause.

Unfortunately sometimes the practice expends more resources and money on a commission than they receive. That is their choice. But sometimes the extra efforts and costs are a result of extra work that was not originally or reasonably expected.

Usually the profitable commissions in the practice will need to subsidise the less profitable and any loss-making commissions.

This balancing will diminish the profits per annum and possibly eliminate them altogether. These profits or surpluses are useful! They may be used for a number of opportunities such as say, in no particular order:

- Dividends to the owners.
- Investing in the business such as with new equipment or training of staff.
- Setting aside as retained earnings for rainy day situations.
- Avoiding going into the red with better cash balance.
- Paying off loans, overdrafts and debts.
- Providing benefits and bonuses for staff.
- Associated tax.

If the practice is expanding all the base costs, using most of the contingencies and more then there will be insufficient funds as profits and some or all of these opportunities will be reduced, suspended or cancelled.

Let's take an example of a medium sized practice with a turnover of £1 million per annum; and an overall profit target of 10% which equates to £100k.

[Some practices may target say 5% or less for profit for dividends (and bonuses) only.]

Let us say there are opportunities to receive another £50k of potential extra fee income entitlement. This is 5% of turnover but 50% of profits. How much of this extra fee will arrive automatically, without great effort, simply by invoicing? And how much will require effort, explanation, persuasion and perseverance? And will it be worth the effort to obtain a suitable return and maintain relationships.

This volume offers guidance and advice on considering such matters and achieving results.

Or to put it another way if the practice were to receive a windfall of £50k out of the blue, by some good fortune, what would it do with the money? Please see list of six indicative bullet points above. And what would one do if that sum were to be in touching distance; one only had to reach out? It may be there! It might be called extra fees for extra work. It may be that close.

CASE STUDY:
More Units.

We received a commission for architectural services for thirty units from a residential developer for a target of planning permission plus handover to a favoured design and build contractor.

We agreed a fee of £5,000 plus VAT per unit. We spent all the fee and did not make any real profit.

We were offered fifteen more units on the adjacent site at the same fee per unit. We accepted.

With some new staff and learning about the sector we were really tempted to "start again" in design terms. But we resisted and made a few adjustments to the previous designs.

In the end this suited the town planners, the D&B contractor, the developer's sales and marketing team – and us.

We made our margin on the second commission plus a bit.

Situation:

We are waiting on the next batch of units – and resolution of their unit fee rate.

1. introduction

Hello. This document provides guidance and tips to management and staff on aspects of asking for Extra Fees for Extra Work and Changes.

The notes are mainly for architectural and other construction practitioner perspectives for individual, conventional client commissions, and yet also for employment in consortia and with Design and Build contractors.

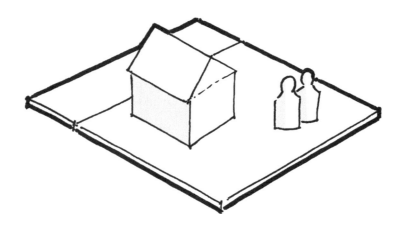

"Was this the base scheme (diagrammatically).......?"

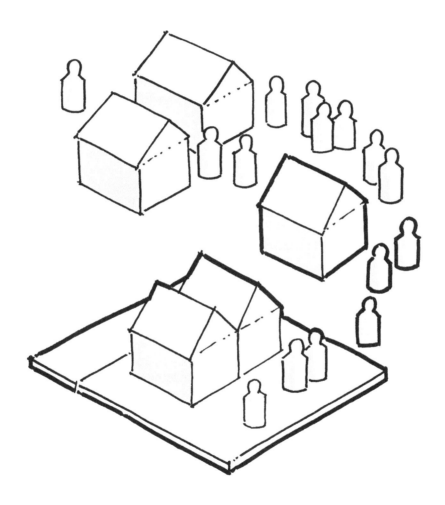

"More Units? More Fees – per unit, sliding scales,
nominally, not at all?"

Each "extra" opportunity for extra fees will require its own specific considerations – one size does not fit all.

The ultimate decision to apply and negotiate for additional fees may rest with senior management – who may sign off or sign the application or meet the customer to resolve.

However, it is incumbent for all project and support staff to maintain an interest and vigilance concerning possible additional efforts – so opportunities may be identified, evidence gathered, records maintained, and applications presented, including possibly in parallel with other parties who may be in similar situations.

In this context "extra fees" includes all additional and extra remuneration including fees, disbursements, expenses and associated taxes that may be legitimately recovered over and above the base sums in the initial setup or in the original agreement. These increases may be due to say scope creep, time extensions, changing requirements, additional or repeated services, etc. as provided for in the appointment and contract documentation or correspondence.

So in section 2 let's get stuck in with some possible situations that incur extra work and so might be available to recover additional fees. So which sound plausible or have been adopted successfully in the past – and possibly may apply on the future?

EXTRA NOTES:

Construction and Total Project Budgets, Scopes and Involvements.

Construction budgets and total project budgets for projects are fundamentally different – and have different impacts in timings and rates.

Construction budgets are usually the predicted contract sum and final account for "the works" to be paid by the client to a main contractor or management contractor, or through a construction manager, or to a design and build (D&B) contractor (who will also receive additions for design fees and design responsibilities).

Total project budgets may include all the related sums the client will pay to others such as: professional fees; statutory fees; surveys and investigations; legal and property costs; furniture, fittings and equipment (FFE); information technology and communications (ITC) equipment and installations; decanting and temporary facilities; public relations and media; marketing and sales; fund raising; recruitment, retention or redundancy costs; contingencies, etc. – plus the construction budget above for the works.

The total project budget can be anything up to half as much as the construction budget, or the same sum again, or more. So if the main fee is to be proposed or agreed as a percentage it can be a really good idea to ascertain to which sum it may be applied. It will make a significant difference!

Usually, where applicable, percentage fees for design team members are based on the construction budget which can float throughout the project duration; or can be converted into a fixed sum at a suitable point in time or stage of the project. Because of this relationship with the construction sum some design team members limit their attentions and contributions to just the construction scope only – and try not to be involved in other total project aspects.

However it is not usually possible for architects and construction professionals to hide away in the construction elements and not be involved in some ways with the other non-construction aspects. And these themes can be interesting and satisfying to address, provide liaison and make contributions to achieve integrated, optimum solutions. That is unless such involvements become excessive, prolonged, demanding in attention and resources and otherwise distracting from the core services – and so might justify additional fees – if excessive and prolonged.

So the options might be:

- To not get involved at all in the non-construction scope (as defined by the budget demarcations) – but that might be unhelpful and unrealistic.

- To set reasonable expectations for such involvements, set equitable limits, apply them – and then withdraw graciously, or if to continue raise the matter of additional fees if to be involved further – which may be accepted, declined or negotiated.

- To get involved, perhaps over-involved – and expect to be paid automatically – and then be disappointed to be refused payment because they thought it was part of your job and you had not said anything.

So are the fees based on construction or total project budgets and what are the boundaries and excesses of involvement?

There are rumours that situations do arise that justify asking for additional fees on commissions.

They may occur separately or in aggregate – concurrently, sequentially or repeatedly.

Certainly we know that only the well-presented cases from a long list of topics will get the best results.

So let's have a look at this long list before we assume priorities.

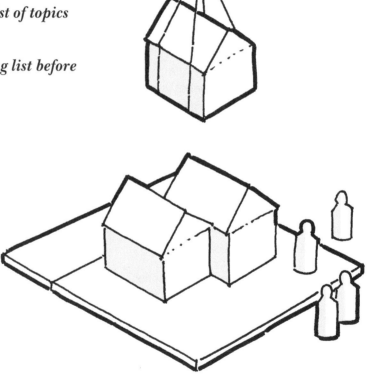

"...and was this the final scheme (diagrammatically)? Any changes? Any extra work?"

The following situations of additional work will certainly not all occur on every commission. So there needs to be an assessment at the start or restart of a commission of which ones are likely to occur and to watch for – and which not. Also which ones might be eligible within the contract documentation for asking for additional fees – and which not. And what are the appropriate clauses within the documentation. A checklist for an assessment is given in Appendix C.

On some projects changes and additional work may arise, however it is not possible to recover the associated costs. So the costs will have to be absorbed or such matters avoided or resisted.

Some of the situations arising may be of such low value that they are not worth pursuing. Or it is decided for political reasons of maintaining relationships not to pursue them. However it may still be worth keeping them under observation with record keeping, to see if on their own or with other topics there is an aggregated situation worth taking up. They may also add to general intelligence, future awareness and possible credits (see section 3).

In all cases it is a matter of identifying if 'extra' work is actually needed and takes place. This will not necessarily be the same as topics which may cause 'non-extra' distraction, irritation, confusion, annoyance, surprise or similar.

Some of the following situations are also shown diagrammatically throughout this volume.

Additional situations may be categorised simply as **scope**, **duration**, **size** or **complexity** (see Appendix B for typical wording).

Here we have adopted seven groupings with over thirty possible topics.

1. **Scope of Works Changes** (4)

2. **Time Changes** (5)

3. **People and Organisational Changes** (4)

4. **Design Changes** (5)

5. **Administrative Changes** (5)

6. **Miscellaneous Topics** (6)

7. **Service Changes** (5)

"Unfortunate or untimely changes of people and organisations can be disruptive and can require efforts to rectify."

2.1. Scope of Works Changes.

2.1.1 Increases in the Construction or Project Budget.

This "extra" scope would appear to be quite straightforward if the base fee is **percentage based**, so the fees will change accordingly with budget changes. That is unless the original percentage fee has been fixed or capped. (Costs can do down as well as up – so will an associated percentage-based fee.)

Note: Percentage based fees can be quite a simple or blunt instrument. For example, clients have been known to ask why should an increase in the costs of a structural or services element result in an increase in architectural fees or vice versa?

2.1.2 More Units.

This scope change can be for more product units or area units or volume units (units can go down as well as up). Will there be the same workload with corresponding same fees for every extra unit, or sliding scales, or nominally, or not at all?

2.1.3 Scope Enlargements.

This could be scope enlargements such as for fitouts to some or all parts of a shell and core scheme, or expansion of external works or public realm, or discovery of particular site or location opportunities – or constraints.

2.1.4 Inflation.

This may be project inflation, as growth or expansion of the building or facility itself. Or this may be financial inflation, which can mean less buying power for a fixed budget requiring efforts to accommodate this erosion or to provide "the same or more for less or even less". Or is there a need to increase the budget to accommodate the cost inflation? Return to top of page if percentage-based fee!

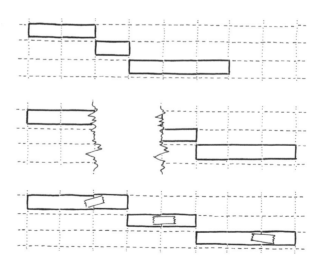

"Delays – as stop:start or stage extensions – can both take place."

24

2.2. Time Changes.

2.2.1 Time Refinements.

Increases or changes of time aspects can include project phasing, changes of priorities or sequencing, sectional completions or partial possessions – pre-site and on site. They may have significant impacts on design and on management – possibly.

2.2.2 Stop : Start.

Stopping or suspending live projects between stages and even during stages is not unusual. When a project stops and then restarts, does this have any impact on the total workload – or not?

There may be consequences of:

- maintaining tick-over contributions during quiet, stopped or stalled periods,

- continuity of staff,

- remobilisation efforts to get back up to speed, especially after long delays;

- and changes or impacts on the work to date – possibly as a result of the cause of the stoppage.

2.2.3 All Stages Taking Longer.

Sometimes it just takes longer to undertake and complete all the stages with their milestones than originally anticipated within appointments or contracts. This may be because the project has grown in size (see Section 2.1.1 to 2.1.4 topics above). But it may be that the target dates were over-ambitious. Even if the project and workload is more or less the same – just over longer periods – are there time-related extra activities and efforts – for example increasing numbers of regular meetings, reviews, reports? These may be compared to say time-related preliminaries within claims from contractors.

2.2.4 One Stage Taking Longer.

When one stage takes or is taking considerably longer than planned are there significant efforts required – or not? Can such efforts be clearly identified, quantified and verified – or not? Will the time slippage or delays need to be made up during the following stages – with acceleration or special efforts?

2.2.5 Acceleration.

Sometimes in adverse circumstances there is minimised critical delay because acceleration, overtime or special measures have been applied for expediency to achieve target dates or ameliorate delays. These may happen in isolation, or multiple times over extended periods, or almost constantly. If there are no-fault, external justifications might the associated costs be recovered as additional fees?

For more information on Expedient Measures and Acceleration see "*Time Matters*" by the author, published by dashdot publications. See Section 9 for more on prolongation.

2.3. People and Organisation Changes.

2.3.1 More People and Organisations.

Does a sizeable increase in the number and involvements of stakeholders and team participants lead to extra work? How much extra work?

2.3.2 Changes of People and Organisations.

Are the departures of existing, then the selections, arrivals and inductions of new parties disruptive – and does this generate extra work or have knock-on time delay consequences? Could this be through bankruptcies / receiverships, sackings or letting go for poor performance, defaults of responsibilities / obligations, poor health, resignations, transfers, promotions, etc. – within the design team, the construction team, the supply chain or on the client side?

2.3.3 More Interaction.

When does interaction become much more interaction, or too much interaction over the norm, which involves extra work and justifies extra fees?

This may be multiple, extended cycles of engagements such as for town planning mutual solutions, or extended statutory difficulties, or utility negotiations.

Or it could be when dealing with stakeholders such as neighbours, special interest groups, prospective tenants or occupiers, etc. over and above their reasonably foreseeable involvements at the time of bidding or appointment.

When things are going on and on and on, how many 'ons' are too many?

2.3.4 Design Team Leadership and Management.

Where the size and membership of the design team increases to such a degree that the management thereof is substantially greater than reasonably expected, or is over a longer period, is there a case for additional fees – or not?

This may apply to core, niche, specialist or trade design contributions, experts and advisors – overall and in permutations for design zones, elements or trade themes.

2.3.5 Changes in Procurement Arrangements.

For example, changes to a two stage tendering approach usually requires more time and effort than one stage. And this may be further complicated by different approaches to two stage. Similarly, clarification may be required in situations for say single party negotiations through to multiple tenderers.

2.3.6 Changes to Contract Arrangements.

Changes between traditional and Design and Build or Construction Management or to some Client Orders may have impact. NEC forms have particular procedures – including when it comes to extras and changes.

2.4. Design Changes.

2.4.1 Design Information by and from Others.

This is when engaging over extended periods or on multiple issues or complex aspects in the preparation, consideration, negotiation and resolution of design information by and from others as consultants or specialist designers – over and above expected editions, iterations and durations. This may also cover "over and above" samples, assemblies, testing, prototypes, etc.

2.4.2 Analysis and Comments.

This can be when presented with tenants' or occupiers' proposals for landlords' approvals – or similar – for analysis and comments – when not obligated to do so in the appointment documentation or has become excessive. Similarly possibly when acting on behalf of tenants and occupiers.

2.4.3 Achieving Alignments.

For example this can occur when retained by a Design and Build Contractor to adjust information within Employers Requirements to fit the Contractors Proposals. Or when a new purchaser or owner arrives and wishes to make modifications and upgrades to an established scheme. If excessive might this amount to extra work which is reimbursable?

2.4.4 Revised Criteria.

During projects, new or revised criteria or brief requirements may occur that may need to be assessed and implemented e.g. for the very latest or expected fire requirements, building standards, town planning orders, pandemic impacts, environmental / sustainability / green issues, adjustments to sector or institutional or marketplace standards or fashions, new technologies or security measures, etc.

2.4.5 Design Iteration.

Usually some creative iteration is a natural expectation within design development when in design stages. However when iteration is problem solving or repetitive or "out-of-stage" is there a case for additional fees – or not? Are tax breaks for research and development also indicators of additional efforts?

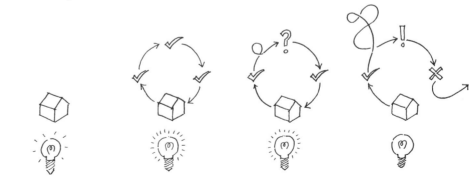

"Iteration – a good idea – unless in excess." (2.4.5)

2.5. Administrative Changes.

2.5.1 More Visits.

Are there recorded site visits or other types of visits in excess of the original numbers or frequencies stipulated in the appointment documents or as might be reasonably expected? Might this include post practical completion visits?

2.5.2 Revising Information.

Are the number of revisions and reissues of information becoming excessive, and for external reasons, which may justify additional fees? Or are they normal design developments and resolutions or correction of internal errors or completion of internal omissions?

This may apply at Stage 4 for Tender Information, at Stage 5 for Construction Information, for Design Intent Information for Others to Design Further, at Stage 6 for Handover Documentation and explanations.

2.5.3 Additional Exercises.

Are there more additional exercises than agreed or expected such as for further value engineering, risk assessments, principals' meetings, retendering or cost reduction – independently or integrated with others? And then implementing the agreed selections through revising, adjusting and reissuing design and other project information (as section 2.5.2 above).

2.5.4 Additional Expenses.

Is it possible to incur additional recoverable expenses, as excluded from or limited within appointment documents – where significant e.g. for travel and accommodation; deliveries and couriers; special printing and multiple copies; special postage and delivery logistics; special photography and video, models, software; provision of space and facilities for group working in short term or over longer periods. These expenses may be associated with other themes for extras or may stand alone separately.

2.5.5 Change Assessments.

If there are change control procedures, notably during Stages 4 & 5, are they occurring more frequently and extensively, consuming resources and expertise, over and above the norm? And then this may lead to the revising and reissuing of information once agreed and adopted (see section 2.5.2 and 3 above).

There is a RIBA Standard form for Change Control, as well as from other internal systems and institutional sources.

2.6. Miscellaneous Topics.

2.6.1 Payments on Behalf of Client.

Sometimes it is convenient or expedient for the practice to place orders and make payments on behalf of the client – and then recover the costs later or up front – possibly with pre-agreed handling charges. This might apply to say model making, surveys and investigations, purchasing samples, travel disbursements for shared trips, subcontract designers or for other specialist services.

2.6.2 Pre-agreed Bonuses.

Might there be a pre-agreed bonus arrangement in place for when the target has been achieved, and value is involved, such that a separate invoice may be submitted?

Might this apply to achieving planning permissions for scope or timing, achieving optimum gross or net areas, or net to gross ratios, sign-offs by key parties, lettings or sales targets, recognition / awards / prizes, energy targets, BREEAM grades, being on or below budget etc. – as pre-agreed. Pain and gain sharing?

2.6.3 Promotional Needs.

Sometimes additional or special promotional material or activity may be requested.

These might be property particulars, images, video and photography, official launches or openings, enhanced handover documentation, submissions for prizes and awards, project monographs, etc.

Sometimes there are commercial or professional beneficial side effects that make charging for such inputs to be churlish or inappropriate – but not always – or perhaps sharing.

2.6.4 Combined, Joint or Multiple Situations.

These occasions for additional fees may be initiated, stimulated or led by other members of the design team or consortium leaders, for collaborative, integrated services which are considered to be "not part of the appointment".

2.6.5 Additional Premiums.

There may be additional premiums for Professional Indemnity Insurance or other insurances for a project above standard levels, durations, depending on availabilities and particulars in the marketplace – to be paid or shared.

2.6.6 The Unexpected.

What are the impacts of unexpected surprises – in theory and in practice? Do they actually require extra work that can be quantified and recovered as additional fees?

Or do they just need working round? Such as pandemics, strikes and industrial action, accidents, material shortages, logistics disruptions, exceptionally inclement weather, Acts of God (and of the Devil).

2.7. Service Changes.

2.7.1 Duties.

Most forms of appointment have lists of core duties and optional duties (for Architects, see RIBA forms). When known to be required certain optional duties can be selected to be included with the core duties and the base fee. Other optional duties may be excluded and are very unlikely to be required. That may leave a third type of optional duties that if they were to be required additional fees are likely to be chargeable and recoverable. It is advisable to be aware of all the core duties – and optional duties (unlikely and excluded).

For example this may be about providing Stage 7 modern post occupancy support and advice (with other team members) including Post Occupancy Evaluations (POE) – although not ticked for inclusion in the historical record or original appointment documents.

2.7.2 Assessment of Claims.

The likelihood of claims by others is unpredictable. So their assessments, when required, are often seen as an additional service. This may be analysis of aspects for extensions of time or loss and expense, by main contractors, responsibilities of parties, quality of workmanship and materials – in order to advise the Contract Administrator.

And there may be the assessment or commenting on claims from other design team members – to advise the client customer.

2.7.3 Excessive Complications.

Excessive complications can be disruptive, distracting and consume resources – and may be recoverable if one is not the source or complicit in their origins. This may require the reinvolvement of internal people who are no longer active on the project, or *additional* resources to be brought in, or senior persons to be involved beyond their expectations or normal allocations or availabilities. Or related to acceleration measures – see section 2.5 earlier.

2.7.4 Additional Efforts.

Might additional efforts to get over the line be recoverable – or is it to be expected to step up and apply "best endeavours"?

So if the environmental criteria or ratings on a project become difficult or enhanced, such as to achieve BREEAM Excellent, does this involve extra work for team members above the norm? Or is it a matter of "whatever it takes"?

Similarly for dealing with rather difficult town planning conditions or new regulations or site circumstances or contractual difficulties?

2.7.5 Contingencies in Budgets.

Are there known contingencies in the project budgets as project, design and construction contingencies – possibly with separate purse holders? Do they also incorporate fees for architectural and other professional services? Are they being spent per stage – and wisely?

What provisions have the practices made in their fee calculations and allocations for each commission to deal with resource underestimation, repeat and abortive work, the unexpected and "going the extra mile"? Can or should this available "lubrication" be expended before addressing "extra fees"?

The above thirty plus topics are a series of prompts. They are more as questions than as answers.

So which may have incurred extra work in the past and the costs were recovered?

Which ones are likely to incur extra work in the future – to watch for and which not?

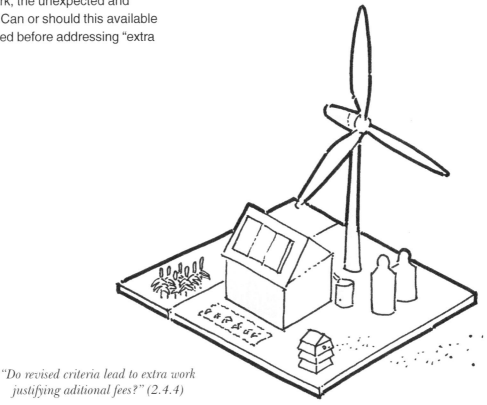

"Do revised criteria lead to extra work justifying aditional fees?" (2.4.4)

31

EXTRA NOTES:

Professional Indemnity Insurance Cover.

Is it possible that architects and other construction professionals become involved in extra situations which are not in their natural skill set, through enthusiasm, helpfulness, naivety, etc, and which take up time and resources?

It has been known to happen!

One way to consider if one is straying too far from one's core discipline and obligations is to ask if this activity or involvement is covered by one's own professional indemnity insurance. If not then it is advisable to back away, explain clearly and get back to your own core discipline.

The same may apply with Quality Assurance systems (QA).

For example this can occur when architects or designers get involved with say master planning, landscaping or furniture design when such services are not mentioned on their website, nor covered by their professional indemnity insurances, nor their quality control systems.

CASE STUDY:
Panic on Reception Tiling – what are YOU going to do about it?

Panic! With only a couple of weeks to go before the reception area tiling was due to start on the critical path, we were informed that the Italian tile manufacturer was in receivership (Exclamation mark) – and asked "What are YOU going to do about it?" (Exclamation mark again).

As enthusiastic architects and designers, keen to please, after two intensive days we were ready to report on similar tiles, alternative tiles, alternative flooring and detailing, plus possible temporary arrangements while matters were resolved – with costs and timings.

At this point we were told that the tile layer had previously been tipped off about the receivership and can confirm sufficient tiles were in his garage and so was ready to go – no problem. No panic.

Situation:

Efforts wasted. Costs not recovered.

Moral of this story:

Before getting too involved or excited with extra work, ask who else has been addressed with "What are you going to do about it?" Or who should be asked?

3. additional efforts as credits

There is a bigger picture to consider. There can be secondary aspects to extra work as 'Credits' as well as or instead of only being additional fees.

Extras and changes leading to additional work and fee issues can occur. But they may not be recognised at the time, or it is decided not to pursue the cost recovery. Either way they may erode the potential profit / surplus / margin for the commission to some degree. Fair enough.

However it may be advisable to keep track of the costs of such "unrecovered" or "unrecoverable" topics and what they may be doing to the financial return, morale and relationships.

Such monitoring will:

- enable one to see if such additional efforts are "going too far" in aggregate in a project situation,

- and if so, they may need attention and restitution.

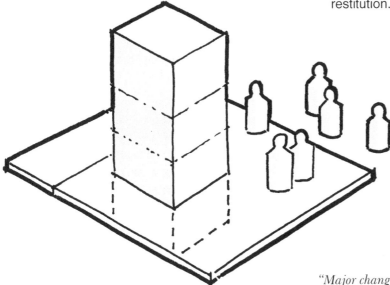

"Major changes can make it a different project – will this be with a new or revised appointment and fee agreement?"

- Also to gain experience for the future so as to notice situations and deal with them or "nip them in the bud" or "put one's foot down – early" – and nicely.

- Also to recognise clauses in appointment documentation that constrict (-) or provide (+) the ability to recover extra fees.

By keeping records or having knowledge of Unasked Additional Efforts and Fees it is possible to use them at the right time as credits in dealing with further requests for services – nicely.

Customers, clients and design and build employers can be forgetful about previous favours and extras when asking for more – or believe it is the norm – and so may need to be reminded – with relevant facts and figures – if they are available – nicely.

CASE STUDY:
And the Client Said…

(As in other Case Studies the numbers below are from a few years ago and have been simplified for storytelling purposes.)

The agreed stage fee was £50k to be paid in ten monthly instalments in arrears = £5k per month. At say £50 per hour per average person, internal charging rate, with 20% margin, this equated to 100 hours per month or 23 hours per week which we took as a project architect for three days per week and some associate director time here and there.

The stage took twelve months. We approached the client for extra fees for the two further months at £5k per month = £10k in total. We did not mention VAT or disbursements – which was probably a mistake, but could have made matters worse.

The client said …that it was the same amount of work just over a longer period – so there was no extra work. And the construction budget was about the same – so there was no extra work. So no extra fees were appropriate.

We pointed out that some of the delays were due to difficulties in getting resolutions with the town planning people. The client said that was not their responsibility, it is part of life and work these days, and we should have tried harder and started earlier on such matters.

We did point out that through our efforts the planners had agreed to some aspects that initially did not appear achievable. The client said …yes and some of these aspects were architect hobbyhorse topics that actually are unproven in contributing to the viability and value of the development.

We pointed out that the extra last two months had been intensive, and we had expended additional resources. The client said …the last two months are always more intensive whatever the duration, that we should know that, and we should allocate our resources to suit the project needs, rather than reflect the invoices / payments / cash flow.

We pointed out that one of the engineering consultants had to be replaced owing to poor performance and this caused some disruption and design adjustments. The client said …yes and the replacements had performed well; also do not forget that the project manager had to speak to the architects a couple of times on their attention and priorities.

We pointed out that we had expended extra efforts to resolve the curtain walling. The client said …that was a good point and thank you, however this was was largely

because of the architect's earlier poor and incomplete designs for this element which had taken longer to resolve and an additional £200k on the construction cost. The client asked …if the architect would like to contribute.

We pointed out that we had spent quite some time with stakeholders on diverse issues. The client said …yes, and it would not have been so diverse if the architects had listened to what the stakeholders were saying and sent someone who was better at negotiation with such parties.

We reiterated that we had participated in Value Engineering workshops in early Stage 4 and Cost Saving exercises in post tender period, we felt we had contributed more design topics and savings than the structural and services engineering consultants. The client said …that if we cared to look such involvements and contributions were specific obligations for all parties in the appointment documents, whether taken up or not.

We pointed out that there had been some exceptionally inclement weather and the contractor had received an extension of time (EoT) of 2.5 weeks. The client said …what has that got to do with anything.

We reiterated that times were hard with inflation and uncertainties. The client said that was true – for everyone – and this development would not make its targeted return. So there were no surplus monies available.

We reminded the client of the earlier discussions concerning if ten months was a reasonable period for the stage. The client said …that the architect was present in the conversations, should have heard what was being said and made suitable provisions accordingly. Also the architects had not mentioned anything about extra fees in such circumstances at the time – and if they had they would have been given short shrift.

We pointed out that the stage had taken TWO WHOLE MONTHS longer. The client said …the fee was lump sum for services for the stage, which for the architects' convenience was paid in monthly instalments, it was not a per month payment arrangement, if the architect would prefer to receive the fee in a single lump sum when the stage was fully completed – well that could be arranged.

We suggested that the client was asking us to take considerable risks related to the project timetable within our roles and responsibilities. The client agreed… and recommended the architects apply good practice risk management techniques to their commissions, similar to those applied to the project, with topics, likelihoods, impacts and mitigations including resource

and money contingencies.

We told the client that we had been projecting a sensible 20% profit margin across these ten months but with a two-month (20%) extension this had been eliminated completely and we would be lucky to break even. The client said …how the architect chooses to allocate the fees on staff remuneration, overheads and other matters was completely up to them. The client would provide the agreed fees, the architects would have to decide what to do with them – before or after their receipt.

We asked what would have happened if the stage had gone on to take say fourteen or fifteen months. The client said …what would have happened if the stage had taken nine or eight months, would the architect have not invoiced for the remaining one or two payments. There was something said about a fair day's pay for a fair day's work. And she said something about cutting cloth and getting acts together.

Situation:

Efforts wasted. Costs not recovered. Lessons learned and applied on other commissions.

4. benchmarking of extra fees

Pay Attention!

- *Extras and asking for extra fees do not happen in isolation.*

- *What is happening on your other current commissions – and then in the wider community of projects?*

- *How are other parties going about dealing with extras and asking for additional fees – as team members, peer groups, competitors?*

- *Overall, what is happening elsewhere?*

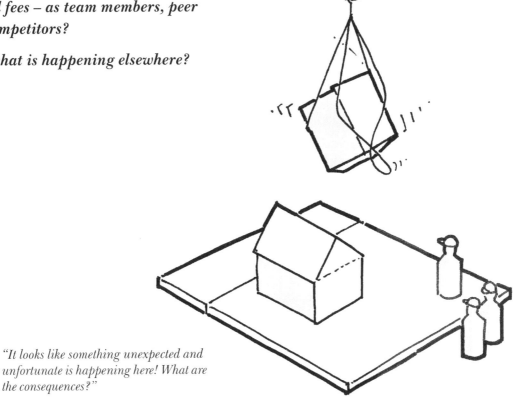

"It looks like something unexpected and unfortunate is happening here! What are the consequences?"

Which of the earlier situations in Section 2 are likely to occur, how are the situations presented and what are the chances of success?

What are the project managers, quantity surveyors, engineers, niche consultants, design and build contractors, general contractors and specialist trade contractors doing about asking for additions including further fees? Do they act as useful benchmarks or guidance; or are they looking to architects and other construction professionals for leadership and guidance in such matters – per project or in general?

What are the benchmarking gossip sources on extras and additional fees in architecture and other construction circles? Is there information available from the RIBA Chartered Practices feedback say on fee growth or fee creep (or shrinkage!) during projects – at start and finish. Is this a topic for the local / regional / national Practice Manager forums or Practice Accountant forums? With discretion, obviously.

What is happening in other industries in relation to additional charges – such as say hotels, airlines, telecoms, health, banking, insurances? Good, bad, progressively, new, not-so-new? Are these likely to be within the experiences of the clients as suitable benchmarks or indicators? It may appear to be difficult to find such market intelligence. But it is interesting that if one's individual and collective awareness is awakened then one does recognise situations, collect examples and share anecdotes.

EXTRA NOTES:

Authorisation to Proceed (Lack of).

Proper, recorded authorisations to proceed to the next stage can be important if one wishes to recover fees, and especially if the next stage were to stall and one would like to recover the fees or expended costs. To have proceeded without proper authorisation may cause difficulties in recovering fees. This will apply to any extra fees as well as the expected / supposed base fees.

These authorisations may be entitled as stage signoffs, gateway reviews, stage gates or similar. Fundamentally such events or processes seek to establish that:

- Everything in previous and current stages has been suitably undertaken and is complete; and if not – what is going to be done about it.

- And everything is suitably in place to undertake and complete the next stage; and if not – what is going to be done about it; and so for the remainder of the project or commission as well.

So on the first criteria, of stage completions, this may include the resolution of any previous requests for extra fees for additional completed work, or in principle for additional work that may still be in hand. Also if there are remaining / outstanding / further activities to complete the stage then the deliverables and resources are defined, and the cost responsibilities are clear and agreed or understood.

On the second criteria, about being ready for the next stage, this involves the consideration by each organisation of known, balanced, fair responsibilities, activities, resources, deliverables, with base and additional remuneration, to participate promptly and suitably throughout. If there are existing agreements and arrangements then these should be checked as remaining valid and relevant. WHEN are you going to do it? What are YOU going to do? What are you going to DO?

If these reviews are not being undertaken openly and project wide, they can and should still be addressed internally within each organisation and recorded in writing.

So whatever it says in the appointment documentation don't bumble into the next stage until authorised to proceed both internally and externally. Don't do it! And also you know clearly what next you are going to be doing. Don't do it!

This can also all be covered by providing and applying QA approaches to the beginning and end of each and every stage progression. Do it!

Conclusion:

Do you want to get started or to get organised or both? It is always possible to get started – and yet not be organised – and then possibly be out of pocket.

Don't let continuity, enthusiasm or pressure overrule common sense, professionalism, sensible procedures and what it says in the appointment. Wait for the proper requested authorisation. Wait. Wait. Wait. Alternatively order more tissues because there could be tears.

5. lessons learned on extras

There is something going on!

In fact there is lots going on!

This section looks for patterns of extras with additional fees and how they might be collected and applied – effectively and efficiently.

Investigate, learn and apply your lessons in your practice – and not just by selective memory and opinion.

"Inflation – of the project, or of the economy?"
What are the experiences and lessons carried over from the last inflation splurges?

Collectively across all commissions in a practice what has been the profile of dealing with extras and all extra fees? Or by sector, location, service, client or client type?

Is it possible to plot the progress of fee entitlement across the stages of a commission for a project – completed or live? Frequently the final fee account is different to the initial agreement or proposal. Usually it is more. Sometimes it is substantially more. On occasions it is less! What is going on? When did it occur? Who has access to this information?

What are your patterns across the stages and for what reasons? What are the sums involved? Could it have been different or more? Was it handled in the optimum manner? Was it worth the effort in terms of the returns and the relationships? Did the requests for additional fees go through like a dream or was it a nightmare and bit of a battle and / or a compromise or have unintended consequences?

Take the last say ten commissions in the studio / practice, and / or a sector, and / or a building type or genre, or a form of appointment or management or client types; undertake an analysis of each commission and then compare for patterns and trends within the types and overall.

It is likely that there will be patterns across and within sectors, clients and client types, job runners and senior managers. What are the lessons? Are they being learned and applied?

A practice orientated questionnaire or interview agenda is provided in section 11.

EXTRA NOTES:

Possible Indicators of Extra Activity.

How is it possible to identify if extra work is taking place which might justify asking for additional fees? Here are a few possible indicators:

To Do Lists.

By studying daily and weekly To Do Lists it may be possible to separate those project activities which are routine or ordinary and those which might be considered as extra or extraordinary.

Deliverables.

If there are obligations to identify "deliverables" for which one has responsibilities, or one finds such an approach useful, then it is possible to identify if there are changes which are directly impacting on the timely and complete delivery of the deliverables themselves, and if there are indirect distractions from "extras" elsewhere.

Information Release Schedules (IRS).

IRSs are for specific deliverables with dates, usually as packages of information for parcels of work – for tendering, or design by others, or "For Construction". Again, are there changes or distractions? Also is it necessary to return to and modify the completed packages of information with 'extras' owing to external influences or instructions?

Timesheets and Design Programmes.

Do the planned and actual activities and staff hours for projects correspond – per week, per month, per package, per stage? And are the corresponding deliverables being delivered – on time? Are there indications of extra work being undertaken – or is it just inefficiency, or investment which will pay off later – or impacts from holidays, sickness, other project obligations, pandemics, etc.? Are the extra topics being recorded separately as they occur? Are the senior staff recording their time involvements with extras?

Drawing Revisions.

What are the reasons for revising and reissuing drawings – do they involve changes and extras?

Written Records.

Are extra work activities being mentioned, addressed and resolved in emails, meeting notes and minutes, change control information?

Have the situations been 'seeded' in the right way in the appropriate media to be referenced and harvested at a later date?

Variations to the Contract.

Are variations issued as instructions – and do they amount to 'extras and changes'? Will they affect the bottom line costs on which percentage fees are based?

Project Directories.

Are the project directories kept up to date? So that at each stage it is possible to see the comings and goings of people and organisations, within natural, progressive growth of stakeholders and participants.

Change Reviews.

An obvious indicator of extras are change reviews and assessments, especially if they are listed or scheduled, so they may be seen individually and cumulatively.

Contingencies.

Are there visible contingency sums? Are they being discussed and spent? Do they involve extras and extra work?

As well as providing prompts on identifying possible extra work do the sources above also provide, good, appropriate, supportive evidence in detail, as a whole, or in summary for extra fees?

EXTRA NOTES:

Demonstrating Value.

It can greatly assist the consideration of a request for additional fees for extra work or changes if some evidence can be shown that some value has been provided. This may be seen within existing documentation, communications or information – which are supportive and can be included or referenced with the application.

If such evidence is not readily available it may be appropriate to provide come context and outcomes to demonstrate usefulness and value.

This may include having a voice, being heard and contributing. Someone may have sat through a "further" value engineering meeting for a "further" two hours and wishes to send in a bill. This will be credible and more likely to be paid if there are records and recollections of the positive contributions and value by the applicant.

These can be counter arguments and counterclaims when the client believes that the actions or inactions of the architect or designer has directly resulted in additional costs to the client and / or loss of value.

CASE STUDY:
The Spiral Staircase.

During Stage 5 we were under the usual time pressure to design the feature spiral staircase which up to this point had been allocated a provisional sum of £25k.

We produced detailed information and under the usual time pressure the QSs came back with a costing of £45k. We were surprised; and the client said this was totally unacceptable and we had better look again.

We took stock, had a design review and went to the trade for some prices, looked at changing the specification and tried alternative stair configurations with quarter and half landings.

After a week we knew the original provisional sum budget was not far off, the specification was appropriate, and any alternatives would cost about the same and have complications.

At this point the project QS confirmed that a junior QS had "priced" our design information unsupervised, under pressure, based on a "similar" other one, but the specification was higher and included breaking out and casting a concrete foundation – that we did not need; and they had not been told about the provisional sum.

It was agreed to proceed with our latest design.

We asked the client if we could charge for our time on this "change assessment". The client said there was no change, and we should take it up with the QS practice. They provided an old-fashioned response and pointed out the number and range of other topics where we had messed them about.

The final staircase was a success and a real asset.

Situation:

Efforts wasted. Costs not recovered.

Moral of this story:

Avoid time pressure situations that can lead to mistakes and misunderstandings. Be early if possible.

6. the key parties when it comes to extras

On the client side who are the key people when it comes to extras? The organisations that may raise or request extras or changes may not be the same as who decide to adopt or approve them – in principle and in detail. And they may not be the same as those involved in resolving responsibilities and payments of extras.

On the design and construction team sides, within the project team, who are the key people to respond and deal with extras and changes with their resolutions? And who are the key parties on the applicant side for additional fees for extra work?

How important is it that there are procedures, relationships and direct, clear lines of communication between these parties – to deal with these issues primarily – and then their consequences?

"Client extras" and the rest.

When it comes to extras on projects it may be advisable to see them in two simple groups:

- The "client originated topics" – as changes of requirements or refinements, additions or improvements for the works or the services arising from or through the client organisation.

- The "rest" – which seem to arise from elsewhere, other than directly from the client.

The "rest" can include:

- Design development
- Site circumstances
- Tender returns and economic changes
- Prolongation of stages and overall
- Stakeholder influences
- Statutory requirements
- Miscellaneous issues
- Combinations of the above.

It will be important for team members if the client has considered all such sources of extras and changes for their project and how they may be accommodated should they arise. For example by risk and responsibility placements in contracts and appointments, by insurances, by reserves and budget contingencies, within business cases, or other, or in combinations – or not at all!

Many clients also have determination to be absolutely clear in their requirements, arrangements and responsibilities for their projects, and completely resolute in sticking to them – consequently there will neither be extras nor the need for changes.

Naturally, consideration of provisions to address such extras for works and services, or not, would have consequences on possible consequential extra fees.

This can also indicate the client's interest in being involved in dealing with and resolving extras – from all or selected or just their own sources.

Spectrum of client interests and involvements.

The client side can vary enormously when it comes to extras between client types, between projects and even changing during projects. The features in this spectrum of client interests and involvements which may come into play on the lines of:

- Is it "THE client" – as a sponsor, champion or owner who signed the appointment and will be meaningfully involved throughout OR is it a "client representative" – as an agent or project manager from the client organisation or from a separate organisation?

- Is it an "Owner" who has real personal interests or dependencies in the success of the project OR are they a "salaried worker" – although their remuneration or career prospects may be project dependant? Who has "skin in the game" – an unfortunate phrase?

- Is the client an individual OR a family OR a business of any size OR an organisation – including local and central government OR an agency OR a charity or voluntary body?

- Is the client an established trading body, with continuity OR a single purpose vehicle – for this project only?

- Is it a simple setup with a single contact OR is there a board or trustees OR non-executives OR advisors?

- Is the client body experienced having undertaken many similar projects OR is this the first time – at all or for this type of project?

- Does the client have expertise of the construction and property sectors OR of other sectors, which provide their reference points?

- Does the client body or its representatives have professional backgrounds, training or qualifications such as chartered lawyers, chartered accountants, architectural / surveying / engineering / contracting / business outlooks – which may affect their ethos, culture or approach?

- Is the project for the client's own use and occupancy OR are they more distant as speculator or spectator?

- Are they available to be closely involved with the project OR will they be more removed owing to location or culture or other predominant commitments, such as busy day-jobs, that restrict involvement and attention? Or for certain days of the week, or periods of the year, or stages of the project?

These features may affect their approaches to their own extras and from other sources – and the corresponding costs.

A MAG Factor assessment will greatly assist in identifying how much help the client will need from members of the project team – with Management, Administration and Guidance. This will indicate possible distractions within the base service; also the possible relationships concerning extra fees.

*For more infromation on "MAG Factor – management, administration and guidance" see '**Leadership in Action**' by the same author, published by dashdot publications.*

True or False Sector Sterotypes

Here are some considerations for sector stereotypes when it comes to additional fees which may be true or false.

Developers in the private sector can appear to be tough when it comes to additional fees. This might be because of the uncertainties as a development. Sometimes they have no or little contingency or would prefer not to spend it at all or on such matters. Sometimes applications for additional fees may be viewed more favourably when a key commercial threshold or project milestone has been achieved, or funding has been secured, or a pre-let has been agreed, or tenants or occupiers have taken occupation. That does not prevent giving notice in writing on additional fees with deferment to another stage or circumstance and then following up. True or false?

Public sector clients can appear to be tough when it comes to additional fees. This may be because the parties dealing with the request are the commercial managers rather than the design managers – who still may have a say. This means they may see and treat architectural and other construction practices as simple sub-contractors – when it comes to additional fees – and possibly for other things. So one needs either to find an alternative route and / or pursue a sub-contractor route with all that means in terms of presentation, pressures and perseverance. True or false?

Private clients for residential schemes, art galleries, studios, leisure premises etc. can be difficult when it comes to additional fees. Even if they are prosperous, they do not achieve and maintain their prosperity by being over generous, without good reason.

Third sector clients in voluntary and charitable fields can be difficult when it comes to additional fees. Their funds may be from diverse sources and be limited. Social factors may come into play. Direct approaches to benefactors may be carefully considered.

As well as these sector features there can also be cultural, social and language differences. This may be seen regionally within nations, between nations and parts of the world, plus those who have an international outlook or multi-cultural appreciation.

In all these cases there may have been "the conspiracy of optimism" so that initial budgets were undercooked – with little or no capacity for "extras" as works or fees.

In all these cases an explanation of the added value, from the extra services leading to the additional fees, is likely to be more favourably received – if possible – rather than represented as duplication, repetition, waste or loss.

In all these cases there may be a better chance of success if the client on the receiving end is not seen as the direct cause of the extra or presented as the party to blame outright – if possible. However honesty counts – and is easier to remember.

Examples of some of these situations are provided in the exercises in Appendix A with the McGivity Conundrums.

Situation:all clients are different in sectors and across sectors.

Moral of this story: horses for courses.

"Was this the expected stakeholder involvement (diagrammatically)....?"

"...and was this the actual stakeholder involvement (diagrammatically)?"

Key Parties in Communications.

Applicants for extra fees can and should consider the key parties from their own side and from the client side – to achieve success efficiently and effectively. This can be addressed via the parties likely to be involved as likely correspondence addressees both ways and so involved in communications – and resolutions.

So here is an indicative circular process with notes to consider:

- Who is the ideal appropriate person as the client-side recipient for the extra fee application and is likely to reply? (Just a single party, multiple parties may cause confusion.)

- And who else on the client side should be copied in – to be informed and aware?

- Who will write the opening and closing paragraphs and sign off the application as the sender?

- And who else on the applicant side will be copied in – including when in group or consortia situations?

(It may be appropriate to copy in senior people, who are not copied in on other day-to-day project issues, to demonstrate the seriousness and backing for the application for additional fees. It also enables them to monitor, support and participate with knowledge and continuity.)

- If the initial correspondence does not bring about a prompt, satisfactory result, is some dialogue necessary – over phones, virtually or face-to-face?

- Who are the best persons to represent the applicant in such dialogue?

- Is this one or more persons?

- Who is the preferred target or likely representative on the client side?

- If the correspondence and dialogue do not bring resolution what is the next stage? Is it presentations, special pleading, negotiations, arbitration – or giving up?

- And who is likely to be involved from each side?

- At which points or thresholds are these arrangements upgraded with a view to a solution being expedited?

And do these points correspond with involvement of commercial managers, or legal advisors, or other advisors or representatives – as advocates or mediators – directly or indirectly – with possible costs?

(In some organisations further parties become involved progressively. This may change progressively in accordance with their game book, experience and circumstances. In other organisations single or limited people are involved throughout all stages.)

- Thinking through these possible stages may influence the first stage of who to correspond to whom with copies. So back to the beginning!

These key party arrangements may be considered for a single application, or for a particular commission or client relationship, or as a common procedure within a practice. The arrangements may be intuitive and informal through to formalised and recorded. The arrangements could be known only on the applicant's side or could be agreed in principle up front with the client side.

On tricky, variable, complex projects with likely tricky, variable or complex change it is probably advisable for applicants for additional fees to identify and monitor the key parties – and recognise that the parties and processes change or may need to change as the project progresses through stages and comes to a conclusion – to achieve optimum results.

7. sources of expertise – for extra fees

Be assured it really helps if you know where to go for advice and expertise pertinent to extra fees.

Know your mentors. Do not expect an easy ride from them. You and the situation will be better for some straight talking.

Asking for extra fees is not something that is usually addressed in formal education or regular training of architects and construction professionals. So the process can appear to be quite daunting and strange – at first.

And what works in one situation might not work in another situation. Sources of expertise can be very helpful to become familiar and gain confidence in such matters.

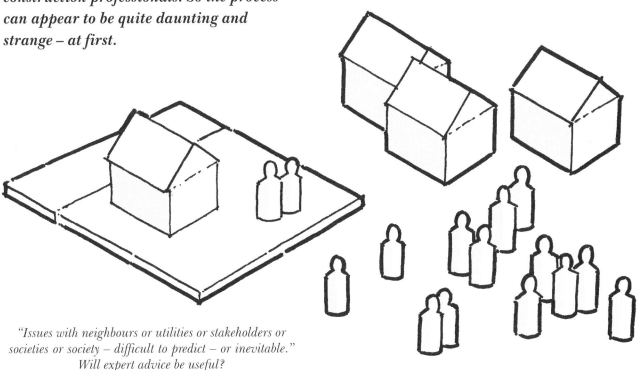

"Issues with neighbours or utilities or stakeholders or societies or society – difficult to predict – or inevitable." Will expert advice be useful?

Assistance can be available in identifying opportunities, assembling suitable evidence, legal or contractual justifications and interpretations, presenting cases in writing and orally, preparing for and undertaking negotiations, and so on in dealing with extras and resulting applications for extra fees.

This expertise may be available internally within the project team, within the studio or within the practice or organisation. Also the administrative functions can have roles to play from within finance and accounts, commercial and marketing, personnel including training, ITC including record information.

External expertise may be available via legal advisors, claims experts and "on-side" quantity surveyors or project managers with such experience. No win : No fee understandings may occur.

Building up expert contacts and knowing when to involve them is a key skill when it comes to addressing extras or changes and asking for additional fees. This includes complex situations – such as joint bid and consortia situations.

Some client representatives have been known to offer advice and guidance on aspects of extra fees – on their projects or generally – occasionally. Listen carefully to what they say and act accordingly – initially at least – usually.

Professional Indemnity Insurance brokers and companies may be interested in additional fees when responding to incoming counterclaims when engaged with insurance liabilities.

EXTRA NOTES:

Preparing Invoices and Getting Paid.

Preparing invoices and getting paid is a regular and important activity for all trading organisations. Timely payments are the lifeblood of all practices. These general pointers on such matters may equally apply in relation to expediting extra fees – or more so. Thoroughness, diplomacy, tact, patience and persistence may be required.

- Establish / verify what will be an acceptable invoice – in form, content, timing for both parties.

- Prepare the valid invoice – promptly.

- Recheck the invoice before sending – and send.

- Note the latest date for payment (e.g. in 28 days).

- Set up protocols for monitoring the process and progress through to payment if required – or just wait-and-see.

- Select monitoring / checking / following up from: wait-and-see, on their receipt of invoice, "soon" after receipt (within one week?), regularly, just before due, when due, after due, well after due – or combinations.

- Select follow-up communication media – face-to-face situations, email, telephone, other – pre-planned or casual – stand alone or with other activity, – or combinations.

- Decide on the applicant's side who is to follow up on invoice payments e.g. the person who signed the invoice application, project staff, senior parties, finance and accounts department, other - or combinations.

- Always be knowledgeable if payment may have been received – before expediting further.

- Ask if "cleared for payment".

- If not – why not?

- Ask who authorises payment and are they aware and available to authorise.

- Is set-off or counterclaim possible?

- What can be done about any bottle necks or difficulties?

- Might this involve clarifications, more explanation, withdrawal and resubmission, devise new application, re-dispatch to others, special pleadings, other – or in combinations.

- Enquire when payment may be expected.

- Ask when to enquire again – and to whom.

- Consider asking for a payment on account.

- Identify who to contact if special attention or special pleading is required or a complaint is to be made.

- Clarify if to invoice in a different way next time – if there is a next time.

- Consider if a payment is not received at all or is excessively delayed or reduced should work activities be reduced or suspended.

- Or to put it another way, decide why work activities should continue at all / not be suspended / cease altogether – if due payments are not being received.

- Be aware of possible escrow account arrangements, pay-when-paid situations (if legal), funding and drawdown criteria and timings, calendar cycles for payment processes with key dates.

- If necessary, apply risk management techniques.

- Identify and involve the internal people who are good at this sort of thing as part of their jobs.

- Before getting too excited, frustrated or contractual about payments, always try to arrange a face-to-face conversation – set up specifically or tacked onto something else.

CASE STUDIES:
Engineering Involvements and DRS.

It wasn't long into the project that we discovered that the M&E services consultant had excluded the rainwater systems from their duties.

The project manager, who had squeezed everyone on fees, informed us that as Lead Designer this was part of our responsibilities. We were surprised!

Pretty soon afterwards we discovered that we were also assumed to be responsible for the design of in-ground foul and surface drainage systems up to sewer connections and design of soakaways. The situation was getting worse!

At about the same time we found that the structural engineer had excluded structural aspects of loadbearing masonry, external works (including boundary and retaining walls) and architectural metalwork such as stair flights and balustrades. Although they would assist – if we paid them. It was not getting any better!

We needed to be careful on the cover provided on our architectural professional indemnity insurance and our in-house competences. So we decided to pay others as subconsultants for such services. They did a good job.

We approached the project manager for compensation in whole or in part, but they were not amenable.

In the end we paid out a few grand that added to our costs and affected our bottom line.

Moral: The moral of this story is that these days for all our submissions or proposals for commissions we thoroughly check and comment on the Design Responsibilities Schedule (DRS), or design demarcation matrix, if provided. If not provided we offer our own schedule and stipulate that all duties and associated fees are subject to agreement by all parties. We usually use primary, secondary and advisory involvements of parties for each element or package or similar.

We found that it is always possible to verify and adjust the original schedule at later stages to suit circumstances – with adjustments to responsibilities, allocation of risks and distribution of remuneration. Circumstances can include adoption of design and build, involvement of specialist consultants, design portion supplements and design involvements of the supply chain

It is worth the efforts. Once bitten twice shy.

EXTRA NOTES:

Change Control.

There are a few aspects when it comes to consequences of extras in respect to changes and change control:

- For resources undertaking change assessments,

- For efforts implementing the changes once authorised,

- And the impact on the construction budget when percentage fees apply.

So some questions and suggested answers:

Q. Change against what?

A. Good question. What is the base condition? It could be against the signed-off brief, the agreed Stage 3 report, the Planning Permission or submission, the pre-tender estimate, the contract documents with contract sum, etc. Therefore it depends on the stage of the project.

Q. Are change assessments usually chargeable?

A. Good question. Not every time usually, unless they are particularly extensive or fundamental, or on multiple occasions, and agreed as chargeable in advance in principal or for specific instances.

Q. How are assessment involvements and costs graded and calculated?

A. Interesting question. This usually involves people resource provisions of hours, days, moving into "weeks" per person involved, using suitable rates per time unit – for inputs from nil, light, medium, heavy and special. Don't forget to allow for special involvements of others where required.

Q. When should implementation costs of possible changes be considered?

A. This should be part of the initial or upgraded assessments of changes and consequently included with the assessment inputs and reports to provide the whole picture.

Q. What happens to the business-as-usual activities, pressures and responsibilities while change assessments and implementations are being undertaken?

A. Important question. They probably are expected to be unaffected and to continue as normal – unless agreed otherwise. Critical delay or disruption is not usually an expected or acceptable consequence of considering or implementing changes. That does not stop it occurring – with knock-on effects.

P.S. There is a RIBA Change form – which covers all of this.

8. working checklist – for extra fees

We have established that asking for additional fees is not something that stands alone or in isolation. It gets mixed up with all the other things that might be happening on a project – sometimes too mixed up.

So these working checklists try to incorporate the bits on extra fees, with all the other bits to provide some context. Over the following pages this checklist is in five sections of:
Setting the Scene (1-4),
Opportunities (5-9),
Approaches (10-12),
In Action (13-16)
and Resolution (17-18).

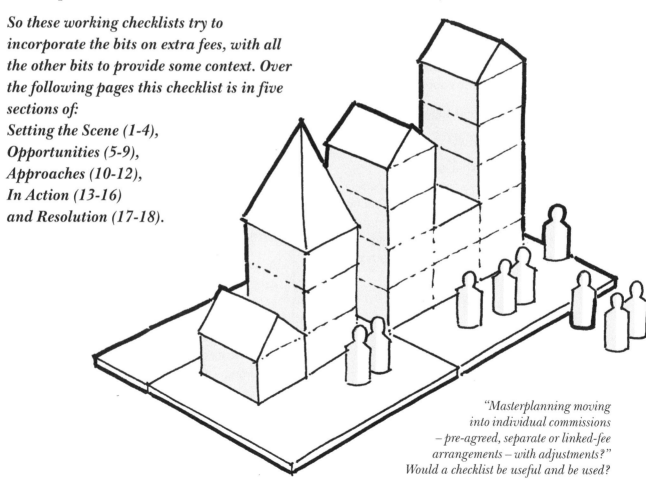

"Masterplanning moving into individual commissions – pre-agreed, separate or linked-fee arrangements – with adjustments?"
Would a checklist be useful and be used?

working checklist – setting the scene

8.1. Checking the Appointment Documentation – also concerning extra fees.

Generally checking of appointment documentation can occur when receiving an enquiry, or putting a bid together, or on receipt of an order, or confirmation of an appointment, or with changes of appointment arrangements.

The checking can be done internally or with external legal and insurance advisors. The checking can cover the terms and conditions and the material within the appendices such as scope, services or duties, programme dates, named parties and fees. Often one is looking for the gaps that need to be filled or clarified, or for onerous clauses such as for liabilities or contributions.

In our case we are looking for matters related to changes, extras and additional fees. Are there clauses which allow recovery of additional fees or restrict the ability to ask for additional fees – such as "fixed" items? Are there opportunities, gaps, weaknesses or ambiguities which might be monitored and possibly used or exploited to gain additional fees? What does it say about prolongation?

It may be useful to ascertain if other members of the design or project team have similar terms and conditions within their appointments and so have similar arrangements for approaching additional fees. This may achieve a level playing field across the team members – in theory; and it may be interesting to see what happens in practice.

Experience and training for looking for such matters in the documentation can be useful. It may be necessary to ask the general checkers specifically about these situations and opportunities for extra fees.

This may become more interesting in consortia bidding and appointments, transfers of client ownerships, with changes of funding arrangements and key stakeholders, nomination and retention in D&B situations, taking over from previous architectural or other incumbents, etc.

Appendix B provides some examples of typical appointment clauses with commentary.

Does the appointment documentation or the fee calculation for a commission contain a project resource schedule or a labour plan or similar? Is it for internal consumption and guidance only or has it been shared with the client? Will it clarify and support planned and actual situations related to resourcing?

8.2. Assessing the Margin.

There is a range of possible margins or returns or surpluses or profitability per commission. Practices do have different approaches.

These may include say: standard profit (at say 5 to 10%), lower profit (at under 5%), or break even (to just cover fixed costs only, with no surplus, possibly for an early stage), or subsidised, or no charge (pro bono or speculative). Or with 'Super Profit' – say over 10%?

So what is the target margin? And where do additional fees fit in?

Is it the intention not to be asking for additional fees because the agreed fee is suitable / adequate / even generous (with some "fat" or contingency to absorb some additional involvements); or are some additional efforts inevitable but whose costs are not worth the efforts or disruption of pursuing; or such requests for additional fees may detrimentally affect relationships with clients or others on this project or for future opportunities?

Or are additional fees a necessity – to make up for losses elsewhere on the commission, or just to cover costs for the extra involvements, or to set a standard so as not to be taken advantage of or be seen as a soft touch?

What is the strategy on asking for additional fees for each commission – will it be from the start – or as they occur during each stage – or at the end? The strategy can always be changed later if appropriate.

8.3. Briefing the Internal Team.

Congratulations, we have won a new commission! Or it is finally getting under way! And you lot are working on it. Hurrah! Exciting!

So the internal team members need to be briefed about the project itself, the commission received and the appointment arrangements. Perhaps the briefing is mainly about the exciting design opportunities and challenges. But at least some team members, and possibly all, are going to need to be told about appointment contents – and the strategies for asking for additional fees or not.

This briefing and review may take place at initiation, key stages, restarts, changes of staff, etc. – and the foci of the briefings may change or be refined each time – possibly including the circumstances and attitudes to extra costs and additional fees.

There may be a tendency to "not rock the boat" in the early stages. Later on there may be greater focus if target margins are not being achieved.

A 'scope and appointment' review with checklist can be a key aspect of internal quality assurance (QA) procedures.

Similarly QA checking that project staff know, understand and have access to appointment duties, services, responsibilities deliverables etc.

Staff buy-in to the management, resourcing and productivity on a profit can be beneficial. However, this awareness is without final responsibilities or authority on such matters – which remains with the principals or designated project leaders

8.4. Design and Project Reviews.

There are the essential design reviews. And then there are project reviews. Internal project reviews may cover aspects of finances, client satisfactions with the project and the professional services, resources for the commission, deliverables and provision of stipulated services – all can be addressed within in-house project reviews.

The financial aspects can be linked to the other management aspects and can cover invoicing, payments, costs, margins – and the situations on additional fees. When might these project and financial reviews take place – monthly, quarterly, stage ends, as requested by upstairs, weekly when under pressure or in crisis? And who is involved? Should the designated job runner initiate, coordinate and record the project (and design) reviews?

working checklist – opportunities

8.5. Response Options to Extras.

Be clear and prompt when getting into unexpected 'change and extra' areas which may "not be part of our job". Raise and discuss internally or seek directions.

The popular approach is the last one – of the chat – for up to 15 minutes. During this conversation between suitable parties it may be possible to:

- Establish the background reasons for the proposed change.

- Clarify the proposed change or permutations clearly.

- Identify the likely impacts or ranges of impacts – including time, cost and knock-on effects.

- Establish the best approach and format of assessment such as a "report" or a "letter" if required.

- Challenge the proposed change to see if it can be adopted immediately – or dismissed forthwith.

There may be options to suggest, consider and resolve or prioritise, such as:

- Not to be involved in the extra aspect at all / in any way. And say so – with no chances of additional income.

- Or to provide limited involvement – without remuneration. With limits.

- Or to be more fully involved – with additional fee remuneration. With agreement.

- Or wait quietly for a week and see how things pan out. Does the change materialise, change or disappear?

- Or seek or await a clear instruction or request. In writing.

- Or continue steadfastly with existing activities and commitments – especially if you are up-against-it to make deliverables available on time.

- Or drop everything else to deal with this additional topic!

- Or arrange to bring in extra resources, work overtime, or displace or defer current activities to accommodate working on the "extras".

- Any other possible responses? What are the precedents on this commission, for this client, or generally in the practice?

"Is it necessary or appropriate to involve others?"

60

8.6. Notifications of "Extra" Activity.

Promptly notify the client or client representative, such as a project manager, where additional activities or contributions are likely, or in hand, which may necessitate or justify asking for extra fees.

Decide if this notification is to be verbal, in writing or (probably preferably) both. Generally follow what it says in the appointment documents.

Have a change assessment hierarchy in place of say a "report" (at say £(000s) cost / charge or more), a "letter" (at say £(00s) cost or charge), or up to say fifteen minutes of "chat" (at no charge) – which may clarify the issue, and/or the approach, or dismiss the issue.

Estimate the reasonable number of each type of such assignments say per month or stage within the base fee so at no charge – as a norm – after which charges may be made.

If the project or commission has particular processes or procedures for dealing with extras and change control e.g. such as NEC arrangements – then ensure familiarity and apply them. Double check that any similar internal Quality Assurance arrangements or good practice is aligned, compatible or suspended – after which changes may be warranted and requested.

8.7. Record Systems.

Set up time record systems for all changes and additional services that **might** be time charged – even if they don't result in finally asking for additional fees. Get into good habits. On time sheets use general or individual suffix numbers to the project number for each extra theme or topic.

Also maintain diary notes or a commentary on such "extra" themes as they arise – to supplement any hard evidence such as correspondence, minutes, time sheets, photographs, design information, etc.. Contemporaneous notes may be helpful at later times to establish circumstances, contexts and for credibility.

Keep records of all change assessments or other "extras" from the start of each stage – not just when the numbers or volumes start to feel excessive or disruptive.

Similarly keep records to be able to assess numbers and timings of drawings produced and issued with revisions for General Arrangements (GAs), for elements, by other consultants, by specialists; numbers of Architects Instructions (AIs) / Variation Orders (VOs), Site Directions / Instructions, Confirmations of Verbal Instructions (CVIs), Technical Queries (TQs); contractors' programmes, etc.

One has to be careful as such information might be open to various interpretations and so might back-fire, so that the case for additional fees is not as strong or persuasive as might have been thought. But that does not prevent the information being collected and recorded for its possible use – in the right circumstances.

8.8. Budgeting – of extra work.

When extra work has been identified or is imminent say something, be prepared to offer lump sums, estimates or ceiling figures (which may not be exceeded without express permission – in writing) – rather than just saying "extra" or "Time Charge" without any parameters. Boundaries may need to be put in place for clarity of scope, durations, inputs or outputs – of extras and changes – so variations or extensions thereto or more extras can be recognised.

By advising on budgets for additional fees for changes the wisdom or appropriateness of the changes themselves may be challenged or called into question.

On most projects there are contingencies in financial terms to deal with the unknown, unexpected, changes and extras. These provisions may be open or secret – as hidden in a "back pocket". It may be appropriate to point out that these contingency allowances may not just cover the direct costs of "extra" works but the related indirect and additional preliminaries, fees, overheads and expenses. Such additional consequences should not be forgotten and should be included, or noted as excluded, within formal change assessments or casual, ballpark estimates of possible additional requirements.

It is important, when dealing with estimates of additional fees or settling sums to be paid, to be careful of rounding off or up or down; or whether to be exact and precise; or provide ranges.

It is good to be clear if these figures need conditioning by saying "including (or excluding) expenses" or "including (or plus) VAT". It could make quite a difference to satisfaction, fairness and disappointment.

8.9. Wider Team View or Involvements – in extra fees.

Be clear if requests for additional fees include or exclude or mention other team members e.g. for architects and designers involving engineering, surveying, construction and management expertise. Consider if this adds strength to any proposals and resolutions for extra fees – or adds complications. For example the need for others to be involved in integrated change assessments and implementations or holistic value engineering reviews and adoptions.

Is it likely that other parties on a project are also likely to ask for additional fees on the same or similar themes? Might some liaison or collaboration with them be appropriate? Or should it definitely be avoided?!

8.10. Approaches to Extras.

Be aware, be vigilant, be precise, be firm, be fair, be honest, be patient, be persistent, be lucky.

Decide on the vocabulary. For example is one "making a claim" or "seeking an entitlement" or "requesting recompense" or "seeking recovery of costs of extra resources" or "dealing with the consequences of changes" or "applying the contract terms" or possibly "asking for extra fees for extra work".

Frequently communications on additional fees are conducted formally in correspondence at arm's length – rather than in face-to-face conversation with explanation, discussion and persuasion. Consequently applications for additional fees may be simply rebutted via correspondence – because the client or customer does not believe they are liable and / or does not want to pay or deal with the issue or feels aggrieved in some way.

It may take resilience, persistence, patience and tenacity to continue to explain to the client or customer their obligations to reimburse additional fees for extra services and work – and the background and merits of the case in question. Usually it is advisable to repeat the original reasoning again, directly and clearly – to get the main message through. Only later present further supplementary arguments or justifications. This stepped approach may require face-to-face arrangements, professionalism and recognition of the likely counter arguments and how to deal with them. Such meetings may be separate and specific or bolted on to other events. This may not be easy – at first. However practice makes perfect, and one has to start sometime. Start with an easy, obvious case with clear available data.

It is probably better to deal with additional fees frequently, promptly, little and often, as and when. This is rather than leaving it all to the end – aggregated, with hindsight – probably. Even if resolution does not occur and payment is not made each time it is useful to put down a marker each time. Perhaps a regular monthly or quarterly statement on such matters would provide awareness and continuity. But this is not always the case and sometimes a single wash-up approach may be appropriate or necessary.

Some architects and other construction professionals prevaricate in asking for additional fees. They may feel that currently is not a good time and a better time will occur in the future – or there is never a best time. So certainly while there may be bad timings with some clients on some projects, it is unlikely there is going to be an ideal, golden time to start asking and presenting a case. If some delay in submitting does seem sensible that should not stop the assembly of the case, so it is developed, tested and ready-to-go – for breaking the news through to a full submission – for when the time is "right".

So consider preparing the documentation as you go, at the time, in a professional manner – for use now or for later. This will also establish the merits or credibility of the claim rather than a vague aspiration. This will also mean that one can move on with other activities without this aspect cluttering up one's inbox or to-do lists.

If there is a possibility of imminent suspension or termination of services, or of the project, it may be advisable to lodge promptly any applications for additional fees.

8.11. Decision Makers.

Ascertain who the decision makers might be on the receiving ends of the client or customer sides for any requests for additional fees. This may vary from project to project, stage to stage on projects, topic to topic for additional fees and the sums involved. Prepare the information in such a way that it may be fully understood and appreciated by the decision makers and by possible advisors or third parties. Make it easy for them to appreciate the merits of the case and approve or accept it. Generally provide a succinct explanation and then add the detail as appendices or attachments.

Section 14 provides a checklist for Extra Fee submissions.

However be prepared for questions and queries, requests for more information or justification, some bureaucracy and administration. Also there may be delays, lack of responses, "lost in the system", "let's wait and see" deferments, etc.

One size does not fit all. All clients are different – and have different approaches to extras. And their attitudes can change during projects.

See section 6 on key parties when it comes to extras.

8.12. Separation of Extra Fee Invoices.

When requesting payments whether the additional fees have been formally agreed, or there are less-formal understandings, or it is a repeat of a similar earlier application for payment – always submit them separately – and not combined with regular or standard invoices for base fees. This is to avoid any possible difficulties or prevarications of the additional fees delaying the payments of the other, basic, regular aspects.

This may mean some additional administration but generally it is worth it – for clarity and simplicity.

This may also apply to additional disbursements and expenses which may be seen as "extra". Alternatively they may be incorporated within regular aggregated recovery of such sums.

With fixed percentage fees there are anticipated payments.

If the construction budget increases so the fee will increase.

And if the costs go up again then the fees should go up again.

Will this be back-dated for earlier stages?!

working checklist – in action

8.13. Keeping the Client Appraised – of additional fees.

Keep the client – at suitable levels – suitably appraised of the situations on fees – including additional fees. It is not necessary to tell senior client persons that subordinate persons are processing applications – unless the processing is taking an excessively long time with deferment, distractions, bottlenecks, difficulties with the application or simply not the availability or capacity to consider the request.

It may be wise not to make a big deal of resolving additional fees – to keep them in perspective – but still in view. This may be achieved by incorporating them into reports and conversations with regular or routine matters – and with the extra services themselves or claims by other parties.

Agreeing to additional fees may not be a familiar or easy task for many clients. It will add to their costs and erode their profits or returns. So some resistance should be expected.

Be aware that requests for additional fees may need to be sent "upstairs" to higher authorities for final approval, authorisation or decision making. Sometimes there are financial thresholds beyond which higher authorisation is required. It may be worth while to ascertain such limits if possible and work within them if possible.

It may be worthwhile informing one's own internal higher authorities also when matters are being escalated and to be on standby for possible involvement.

When there is a resolution, whatever the outcome, it may be advisable to express thanks and satisfaction in a professional manner – to close the matter – until the next time. This may assist to maintain good working, commercial and social relationships. Alternatively if the answers are unacceptable then decide promptly how and when to respond. Don't let resentment or other emotions build up. On the other hand don't send some off-the-cuff, knee-jerk reaction of frustration or disappointment.

8.14. Hope Money and Hopeless Money.

Be aware of hoping that it may be possible to recover additional fees, but the case is by no means certain or legitimate. This can happen on difficult commissions that are frequently time and / or resource consuming and are **not** achieving their planned margin or are even making a loss, including for the client customer. Such hope fees can be devised to save face of internal bid or project team members and divert criticism of real or perceived performance.

It is possible to leave such hope money "on the books" for some time and until it becomes self-evident that the cases for additional fees are not coming together or not for the hoped-for amounts. This may be some way down the line – and when hopefulness can turn to hopelessness.

Alternatively when a difficult commission later comes out well in design, function, budget, timetable and accolade combinations then perhaps the environment will be better to approach asking for additional fees – with reasonable chances of success.

8.15. Counterclaims and Set-off.

Sometimes applying for additional fees can stimulate a counterclaim and set-off.

A counterclaim is a claim by the other side. In the case of architects and other construction practitioners the client may claim that not all the services have been fully or well provided. Or that the architect or others are at fault, and this has put the client to trouble, loss and expense. In such circumstances the client may seek to recover their costs and so present their own claim as a counterclaim – against the base fees or the additional fees.

The client fee credit assessment may then be set off against the fee invoices – in timings and methods set out in the appointment documents or in accordance with statutes. This response may result in a discounted or totally negated invoiced sum – which was not the intention!

It may be advisable to try a "small" request for additional fees on a discrete topic to see if it is settled or results in a proportionate or even disproportionate counterclaim. This may set the scene of future outlooks and arrangements.

A large request for additional fees may result in a large counterclaim by stimulating the client to consider such matters as performance and fault which may not have arisen otherwise. At this point the original request may be invalidated, dismissed or withdrawn – leaving the counterclaim still on the table – with consequential loss of potential income, efforts and costs of responding to the counterclaim, and additional costs in settling the counterclaim. So an ill-considered application for additional fees can "open a can of worms".

From the other direction some clients or their advisors may be particularly aggressive or litigious and indicate that they may raise contractual and performance issues by team members leading to counterclaims – to dissuade and reduce additional fee applications, entitlements and payments – whether base or additional. In such circumstances assembly of claims for extra fees may be advisable to assist with possible disputes, negotiations, resolutions and settlements – with or without maintaining reasonable amicable relationships.

8.16. Counterclaims and Complaints.

Are the topics for counterclaims from those receiving applications for additional fees likely to be similar to the themes of complaints arising from the same parties?

For example complaints to the Architects Registration Board (ARB) fall into the following categories:

1. Failure to provide a clear written contract for professional services.

2. Failure to confirm the price to be charged for services.

3. Matters related to planning applications.

4. Inadequate budget and cost advice.

5. Failure to manage tendering procedures.

6. Contract administration.

7. Technical matters related to design and production information.

By far the most common complaint concerns the first theme. Other professions may have some similar and other themes.

An internal review of complaints, concerns, disputes, etc. will indicate if there are any alignments with counterclaims, offsets or contra-arguments when asking for extra fees.

A review with professional indemnity insurers (PII) or brokers can also assist with identifying any alignments.

EXTRA NOTES:

To tell the (best) story.

What is the best media to tell the story to secure extra fees for extra works with clarity and confidence? Options might include:

- text – clear, unambiguous, fact-based, narrative and explanations, persuasion and truth,

- numbers and figures – with calculations,

- illustrations, charts, models, diagrams – summarising before and after or planned and actual (see within this volume for possible inspiration of illustrations),

- contemporaneous material and records – as appendices, attachments, references.

- combinations of above.

  A checklist for extra fee submissions is provided in section 13.

8.17. Methods of Resolution.

Sometimes a request for additional fees can become a dispute or a stand-off. It is good to know in advance the methods of resolution within the appointment documentation and if they will apply when asking for additional fees. See Appendix B for some examples of clauses on resolution methods.

So what might be the options and preferences from say dialogue, mediation, adjudication, arbitration, county court debts, offsets and counterclaims, sources of expertise and legal advice for these routes – and negotiation within Alternate / Appropriate Dispute Resolution (ADR)?

Even 'simple adjudication' or small claims court are still going to take time and consume energy.

8.18. Negotiation.

Negotiation is a skill. Some people have better negotiation skills than others. Even if individuals or organisations appear to be natural, willing and able negotiators, they are still likely to have had some training and practice. So if one is likely to be involved in face-to-face representation to a negotiation on additional fees, or in the back-up, it is probably advisable to get some training and undertake some practice or simulation – in advance.

For particularly large sums of additional fees, when the parties are wide apart, there may be a case for negotiation by mutual agreement – whether it is mentioned or not in contract or appointment documentation.

There are some general rules and guidance that apply to all negotiations and can be used for additional fees. Tips and tricks can include: to agree the arrangements in advance – on format, venue, timings, topics / scope, representation; to be represented by at least two prepared people each; to identify separate, key aspects – within the bigger picture; negotiate on each aspect; seek win:win outcomes – overall: deal with all the issues on the table; maintain professionalism and cordiality; write down the agreements; if money is involve resolve when and how it will be transferred; etc.

In group actions, with more than one party on a side, the arrangements can be quite tricky including who will attend, in which roles, with what aims. This includes when insurers for Professional Indemnity have become involved.

The five stages of negotiation are usually:

1. Preparation – of the case and also understanding the underlying motivations, with wants and needs of the parties, as well as their views.

2. Information Exchange.

3. Resolving – with bargaining – and trade-offs.

4. Concluding – as agreeing – or escalating.

5. Executing the agreement – with records, actions and consequences.

Mentors can help with following this process – with preparation at the beginning.

Good negotiators have attributes including:

- Thinking ahead.
- Prepared to say "NO".
- Recognising long term relationships.
- Good communication skills.
- Technical competence.

Mentors can help with developing and applying these attributes. See Section 11 for Negotiation Mentoring, or 'NegMent'.

Architects and other professionals may have different roles or interests around negotiation on projects and at the same time:

- as a facilitator of negotiation to reach agreement between two parties e.g. client side and contractor side when in the role of Contract Adminstrator or professional 'good guy'.

- when an observer or advisor to negotiation by others – in the project's interest – to move things along

- as participant with own interests, for example when asking for extra fees.

Culture can have a large part to play around negotiation – across regions, nations, parts of the world plus across sectors – see page 48.

For those interested there are volumes of training and guidance as books, courses, podcasts etc. on negotiation, influencing, conflict management, dispute resolution, etc.

"Report? Who? Me?!"

CASE STUDY:
Reports and Reporting.

They said: "*We need your report for the Friday meeting.*"

What is a "report" on a possible change or extra? Is it an expectation of "a report" as a noun, such as a document, which may be comprehensive, thorough, based on extensive research with structure and recommendations?

Or is it a request "to report" as a verb, as a verbal explanation which may be short, sharp and conversational?

Or is it to be expected to undertake all the comprehensive noun stuff with the hard yards and yet to provide a succinct spoken summary as a verb – as in 'cut to the chase'.

In other words, just to be clear, to respond to the above request, who is reporting on changes, to whom, on what, when and in which format?

This might also be relevant to 'reporting' on extra fees.

Situation: we wasted a lot of time preparing report documents or making them presentable when something simpler would have sufficed – including for 'extra' topics.

Moral: measure twice, cut once.

9. prolongation – and extra fees

Sorry about the prolongation to get to prolongation.

Prolongation is the "extension of the spatial length of something" – in our case this is time. For extra fees purposes prolongation may be considered in three ways of 'between stages prolongation', 'within stages prolongation' and 'overall prolongation'.

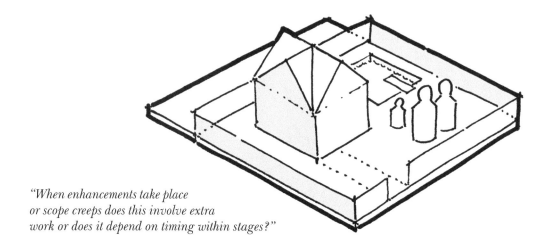

"When enhancements take place or scope creeps does this involve extra work or does it depend on timing within stages?"

9.1. Between Stages Prolongation.

Sometimes project stages are shown sequentially, with continuity, waterfall style. But life is not aways like that. There can be stutters, stagnation, delays and gaps as it may be difficult to complete one stage and move seamlessly onto the next stage.

Examples might include:

- The stopped period after a feasibility study, or viability study, or concept design – say after Stages 0, 1 or even 2.
  This period between stages can appear to be a "quiet time" but in fact it is when the client side and development team may be working at their hardest to bring things together, make deals, complete purchases, secure funds, satisfy key stakeholders, etc. There may be some tick-over support by architects and other construction professionals expected or needed – and possible extra work may be required. Whether this is substantial enough to justify additional fees will depend on requirements and circumstances.

- The period after the town planning application has been submitted and until a satisfactory outcome has been achieved.
  This idealised waiting period can be prolonged beyond the norm or reasonable for administrative, technical or political reasons. Again tick-over contributions and more may be expected until the next stage is authorised. There may be an option to work during the planning or other approval processes in anticipation of a favourable outcome. Sometimes this is called "working-at-risk" because there is the possibility that the outcome will not be favourable, or completely favourable or timely. In which case there would be some abortive work that would need reworking or simply abandoning. Clearly a resolution is required on who might be paying for such reworkings, lost workings or extended activities.

- At the end of the preconstruction period and before the construction stage is authorised to commence.
  This period may be prolonged by such matters as waiting for vacant possession, or services terminations, or fulfilment of pre-start conditions, etc. Again it may be a tick-over period for an architect or designer point of view. But this may change if there is involvement in resolving matters such as if there is a cost reduction exercise when tender returns exceed pre-tender estimates or budget availabilities.

Naturally if original appointments are limited time-wise, do not flow across stages and are purposefully separated then there is no prolongation on these grounds. Similarly, there may be clauses in the appointment documents restricting the impact of prolongation on extra fees.

9.2. Within Stage Prolongation.

Within stage prolongation can occur during any stage when the actual duration exceeds the planned duration. Sometimes the planned duration can be short, compressed or optimistic for an under-defined quantity of work.

This condition can be verified by finding if there is capacity to shorten even further. So can a stage of a ten-unit duration be undertaken in nine, eight or seven? Or is it more likely to stretch to eleven, twelve or more? The situation can be eased if the workload is reduced with fewer activities and deliverables. Naturally extra work within the stage may exacerbate any duration unless special or expedient measures are adopted.

[For an exploration of **Expedient Measures and Acceleration** there is "*Time Matters*" by the author, published by Dashdot Publications.]

The differences between in-stage design development or iterations on one hand and extra work on the other can be subtle. Approaches to "design it once" can clarify such subtleties but may be oversimplistic. Out-of-stage change or variations to briefs, signed-off designs, permissions, placed contracts, etc. may be easier to identify.

However not everything is cut and dry. For example when on-site in Stage 5 there will be continuing design-related matters to be resolved such as town planning reserved matters, provisional sums, provisional designs, design development by specialists and trade contractors, site

circumstances, approval of samples, etc. It is inevitable that some of these matters are going to involve change and extra effort – but whether they are enough to prolong the stage or justify additional fees will depend on circumstances.

EXTRA NOTES:

Planned & Actual – Elasticated, Stalled or Incremental?

When prolongation takes place does it mean that the planned activities, and the allocated resources to undertake them, can simply be "stretched" across a longer period – like elastic?

Or will it be appropriate to suspend activities at no, some or notional cost?

Or does it require incremental extra plant, materials, management and labour to do the same amount of work (or more), over the longer duration – with associated extra costs?

Or might it be combinations of all – depending on the cause of the prolongation, the stage of the project, or the types of resources required to respond to or contain the prolongation?

Can these matters be shown graphically? Can any additional costs be recovered as additional changes?

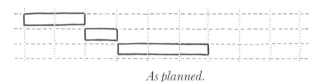

As planned.

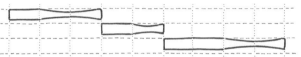

E.G. Actual with three stages of elasticated prolongation.

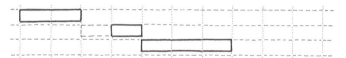

E.G. Actual with one stage of stalled prolongation.

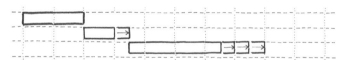

E.G. Actual with two stages of incremental prolongation.

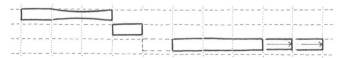

E.G. Actual with combinations of prolongation.

9.3. Overall Prolongation.

It is interesting how most developments and construction projects are not delivered to the time targets initially conceived. Therefore the overall project durations may not be the same as the appointment durations. The delays are combinations of between stage prolongations, within stage prolongations, scope creep – and not forgetting optimism bias.

Often these matters are individual and small scale with small scale impacts, yet can be insidious, cumulative and significant in aggregate. So to assess prolongation one may need to look at the cumulative big picture as well as the individual, small detail.

This may involve monitoring the critical path – if it is readily apparent – and how it may be adjusted or rerouted during the course of the project.

9.4. Critical Path and AFDORPS.

The critical path is the sequence of activities which lead to the shortest possible overall duration. It is often represented by a red line flowing through critical items on a bar chart with network logic, with "end-to-start" direct relationships and restraints. This tends to be most prevalent on Stage 5 Construction programmes of on-site activities as elements and trades with milestones.

Consequently a prolongation topic needs to be critical or near-critical to show true prolongation and delay – which directly may cause additional costs.

Pre-site activities can be just as important for delay as those on-site, if not more so. But the critical path can be more difficult to establish and maintain. These may be tackled through AFDORPS – which may apply to a whole project but more likely to elements or components from a design point of view, or trade packages and parcels from a construction or contractor point of view, notably for managed forms of contracting and two stage tendering. Aspects may be seen in Information Release Schedules (IRS) and Procurement Programmes notably in Stages 4 and 5. This acronym stands for:

A.   Agree Brief / Scope of parcel.

F.   Freeze Design – for parcel.

D.   Deliver Design – for tender purposes for parcel.

O.   Out to Tender – despatch tender enquiry to tenderers.

R. Return of Tenders – and analysis for parcel.

P. Place Order for parcel.

S. Start on Site with parcel.

In this instance it is interesting to assess if delay may have occurred in any one or more of these stages, the reasons for such delay, if they have impact or may be recovered or are not critical. Therefore it is possible to see if prolongation is involved or extra work needed to solve the matter arising or to avoid prolongation.

[A full explanation of **AFDORPS** is provided in "*An introduction to and study guide to COLLABORATION for contractor contributions to design team activities*" by the author, published by dashdot publications.]

"Keeping on the critical path can be tricky."
(an illustration by Rob Dee from "*Time Matters*" by the author.)

10. internal research

If you think you know the answers already you might want to skip over this section.

Or this might be where you should start!

In a data hungry society this is about data.

Alternatively if you have five, three or one year plans those might be the intervals to undertake this research and analysis – to help plan and manage the future – in the real world.

So, this section covers some possible internal research within a practice to gain information on asking for extra fees for extra work.

The research could be centrally coordinated by a researcher by issuing and analysing questionnaires or via interviews or in workshops or combinations.

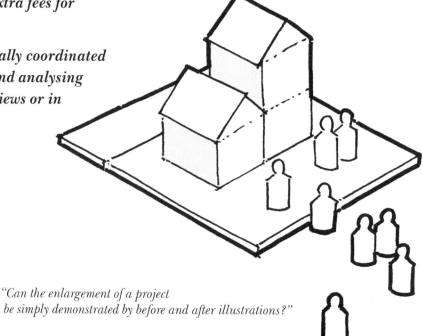

"Can the enlargement of a project be simply demonstrated by before and after illustrations?"

CHECKLIST for internal research

The questions, prompts or topics per commission could be on the following lines:

Q01. Has the theme of asking for additional fees for extra works already been addressed for this project and therefore information is readily available and where?

Q02. What were the original and final (or current) construction values – with percentage change – and commentary to explain, if available?

Q03. What were the original and final project durations from the appointment start date to Practical Completion (PC) or date of termination – with percentage change and commentary to explain, if available?

Q04. What were the initial expected fee (as in proposal / initial appointment) and that finally achieved (as overall invoiced) – with percentage change? Be consistent with disbursements and VAT.

Q05. At which stages and for what reasons did the fee change? i.e. what were the 'extra', or reduced, works or services and what was the additional, or reduced, fee for each?

Q06. If known, what were the original and final profit margins for the project – as sums and / or percentages – as income over expenditure (mainly as resource costs plus overhead).

Q07 What were the general cultures and achievements for recovery of additional costs and fees on the project – as by other consultants, for extensions of time, recovering loss and expense, etc. – as well as for our own fees?

Q08. What could have been done better or differently in relation to the appointment arrangements and documentation and the initial fee proposals in relation to the recovery of additional fees?

Q09. For this project, who were the main players on all sides in relation to additional fees?

Q10. Are there any further comments or contributions you would like to make on this theme? E.g. allowances for extra efforts, on timing of applications, periods and methods for resolution, processes and procedures, missed opportunities?

Q11. Would you be prepared to be an advisor or mentor to others facing similar opportunities and challenges related to asking for additional fees for extra work?

Thank you.

Please return you responses to xxxx.

Are these questions that the mentors may ask and the project staff may anticipate?

11. possible pitfalls around extra fees

We know it may not be an easy ride.

In this section we identify fifteen possible pitfalls or risks that may need to be considered when asking for extra fees for extra work.

These pitfalls may result in delayed or negative responses and so the overall resolutions, detrimental impacts on relationships, distractions from more profitable works, internal tensions, etc.

"Was this on the risk schedule for likelihood and impact? Any consequences? Insurance claim? Including for extra fees?"

Possible pitfalls or risks concerning asking for additional fees at a project level can include the following:

- Junior or inexperienced or administrative staff assembling and dealing with claims for additional fees when they do not know the processes, the project, the circumstances, the background or the client well enough.

- Senior managers and practice owners – ditto.

- Assembling and dispatching a claim without others in the practice checking fully and being given the whole materials and time to comment.

- Not using the time recording arrangements fully and accurately – including for involvements of senior persons.

- Allowing the Accounts Department and others to assume that simply because a job number suffix is in use that the costs will be recoverable.

- Assuming the client contact or someone else is dealing with an application they have received, but no-one is.

- Assuming a client contact has briefed their boss or successor on a claim, when they have not.

- Not having devised liaison or pressure strategies or policies to obtain a favourable decision or response e.g. maintaining decent working relationships, undertaking obligations thoroughly and efficiently, suspending further extras or favours, strict administration, everything in writing, motivated or demotivated people, disinterest in further work, dispute resolution routes, etc.

- Settling a claim on a full and final basis or similar, only to find missing, further or continuing aspects.

- Senior representatives meeting but not adequately briefed on the project and on the additional fees to achieve suitable progress or satisfactory resolution – including being overly diplomatic and soft, or pragmatic and considered, or aggressive and undiplomatic.

- Not allowing for nor expecting some negotiation factors – such as discounting rates or sums, rounding down, splitting the difference, absorbing other possible claims, changes of personnel or procedures, etc.

- Alternatively allowing for or expecting some kind of negotiation or settlement when the other side sees it in principle of necessity or responsibility or 'allowability' – with shut out.

- Not being clear on resolutions and how and when payment may occur.

- Involving insurance brokers and PI cover too early – or too late.

- PII insurers looking after their interests rather than those of the architect or designer.

- Requests for extra fees stimulating counterclaims and set-off – leading to disputes – see section 8.15.

- Colleagues in group actions having different agendas and expectations – reflected in their contributions.

- Upsetting the client and worsening the relationship by poor approaches to additional fees including poor and mis-timed communications; apparent obsession and close attention to commercial positions; pedantic / legalistic / contractual / monetary outlooks.

- Predictably or unpredictably, clients not paying the last invoice of the base fee and it being too late to assemble the case for extra fees.

- Being fearful of asking for extra fee entitlements because it may jeopardise the chances of receiving further commissions or supporting references.

- Not having / being aware / fully using the internal complaints procedure, within QA systems, to deal with counterclaims – and thus keeping matters separate.

- And more. And so on.

EXTRA NOTES:

"NegMent" = Negotiation mentoring.

- Informal, semi-formal and formal giving and getting of support, guidance, directions and encouragement,

- to those makng the case, being in the frontline and on the spot representing the practice,

- in negotiation, problem-solving, firefighting,

- including for extra fees,

- via experienced / opinionated / helpful / available gurus

- from internal (and external) sources,

- as individuals and panels

This role of critical friend or friendly critic can extend to simulating or representing the other side and their possible responses.

"Is there a "NegMent" panel to support, guide, direct and encourage on extra fees?"

12. inducting awareness of extra fees

Who is on the case?
Who is paying attention?
Who is getting results?

*In this section we will investigate some
possible ways of inducting awareness in
staff in practices with nearly twenty
optional suggestions.*

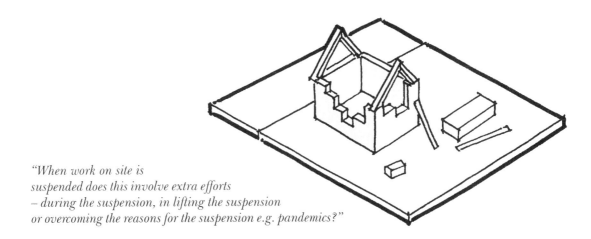

*"When work on site is
suspended does this involve extra efforts
– during the suspension, in lifting the suspension
or overcoming the reasons for the suspension e.g. pandemics?"*

How can a balanced culture of being aware of the significance and opportunities of additional fees be stimulated in a practice? How can this be done in the right way to fit the overall ethos of the practice? Is this a gentle awareness without being an obsession? Or is this an enthusiastic entitlement?

It probably starts from the top, from the directors or holding company / owners; and the directors themselves can have different views between themselves – overall and on the projects of which they have personal knowledge or involvement.

Some people think that extra fees on other commissions should be pursued fully and with vigour. While on their own commissions, matters are more subtle and their approach diffident.

Is the subject of extra fees something to:

- Mention in an interview of potential staff members, depending on the grade, for their awareness, involvements or achievements in such matters?

- Incorporate in job descriptions – depending on the grade?

- Include with initial inductions of new staff or people re-joining after an absence?

- Review during and at the end of a probationary periods of new staff or when promotions occur?

- Address as part of annual staff reviews?

- Identify as a criterion in promotions – to senior positions involving such matters – and within next job descriptions?

- Reward job runners who make their targeted fees and margins, including additional fee achievements where appropriate – with promotion, better projects, further benefits, or even a bonus – if that is fair and proportionate?

- Recognise – say with an annual internal prize for outstanding performance or achievements in such matters?

- Celebrate and announce achievements on profitability of commissions including additional fees – openly or discreetly?

- Provide training as an internal course or courses of study or CPD talks or external courses, events or conferences? – including this document!

- Include situations or exercises related to additional fees when possibly training on leadership, general negotiation or settlements of disputes – including McGivity Conundrums – see Appendix A.

- Make real examples and lessons learned available as case studies?

- Mention or explain in Practice Handbook, Staff Handbook, procedures and processes, Quality Management Systems, etc. – with proforma material?

- Cover as an agenda topic in regular project reviews and reports – for selected or all commissions?

- Be part of practice plans as part of income and profit targets or KPIs?

- Have a clear theme for additional fees, with names of expert champions, in internal Sources of Expertise, or as a Helpdesk, or a guru, or "NegMent"?

- OR avoid talking about additional fees for extra work because it may divert talented people from their focus on client-satisfying, fit-for-purpose, award-winning, excellent design?

- Or avoid because open discussion of hour or day rates per grade and practice profit levels may be over-illuminating or divisive.

- Any more aspects?

13. a checklist for extra fee submissions

At last! This section includes a checklist and prompts for the possible structures, headings and contents for a submission for additional fees.

This may be:

- *In advance of extra work – for resolution, agreement or authorisation to proceed — and to be paid. This is usually the recommended route.*

- *In retrospect – during or after extra work – for consideration – hopefully with resolution and payment.*

These prompts may assist the assembly of:

- *A narrative document for submission and consideration – attached to a covering letter or email.*

- *A presentation with slides.*

- *An agenda for dialogue – with supporting data.*

- *Evidence in a negotiation.*

Software to assist these activities may include such as:

- *Word for text.*

- *PowerProject for time information / scheduling.*

- *Excel for spreadsheets for activities, resourcing and fee calculations*

- *Or combined project management software.*

CHECKLIST for extra fee submissions

Project Title and Reference – in full.

Topic Heading of Extra – clear, unique, unambiguous.

Date, Source and Version Control.

Contents List – from below including appendices and attachments.

Executive Summary – with a brief description of the project, the parties, the issues and the proposed resolutions. Alternatively provide an Introduction here and Conclusions and Recommendations later.

Background – explanation of the appointment and the pertinent contract clauses to the issues under consideration.

Scope of Extra Services – section headings with itemised tasks and quantities. For consistency and clarity the same sections and tasks may also be used in activity lists, scheduling, resourcing and budgeting – as follows later.

Select from say:

- Scoping of Extra Work / Briefing on Issues / Workshops.

- Stakeholder and Client Engagements.

- Related Surveys and Investigations.

- Related Research – including for new Regulations or Standards.

- Meetings and Reports – types, numbers, records.

- Concept and Detailed Design Studies and Outputs.

- Contributions to Change Assessments.

All the above may include involvements of other parties from design team, construction team, supply chain, statutory bodies and client team.

Schedule – timelines to undertake the above extra scope of services – and achieve resolution.

Resources – staff and management to undertake the scope of services to the timeline – by grades.

Extra Fee Calculation – including the basis of the calculation e.g. pre-agreed hourly or daily rates per grade; with resource units as predicted or historically incurred or estimated, with inclusions and exclusions plus methods and timings of payments.

Conclusions / Recommendations.

Appendices and Attachments.

14. non-cash benefits and rewards

It's not just about money!

The main thrust of this document has been to obtain appropriate "extra fees" – in financial terms.

Sometimes this may be difficult to ask for or to receive as cash.

This section looks at some non-cash benefits and rewards that may be available and appreciated by both sides, as well as or instead of direct payment of money.

It is possible some clients (as employers) may be in positions to provide other benefits or rewards, which have nil or low cost to them, and may have value to architects and construction professionals (as service providers). Such additional matters might be offered or requested as part of settlements or in negotiations. They may occur in normal activity as well.

"Can exceptionally inclement weather cause disruption and delay leading to extra work? OR is assessing applications for extensions of time (including for inclement weather) an extra service – with additional fees?"

Some diverse examples which clients or customers or "parties on the other side" may agree to provide or arrange might include those in the checklist opposite, in no particular order...

CHECKLIST for NON-CASH BENEFITS AND REWARDS

- Keeping in the hall stand copies of the project data sheet for the tasteful house conversion and architect's brochures, to offer to guests and visitors showing interest.

- Similarly at reception desk of completed commercial premises, or with the building manager.

- Agreement to be a feature in the property or business section of a local paper or other broadcast media, with credits to design team and construction team.

- Agreement to and contribution to feature in design / construction press.

- Agreement to showing round other prospective clients for the consultant's services as examples of talent – hopefully with positivity and pride.

- Agreement to a feature about the new premises, with video, on client's own website with credits.

- Provision of a front-page image of project or people on corporate magazine or newsletter and interview with architect and/or other professionals – plus contractors, specialists and advisors.

- Agreement to enter for "client of the year" award or similar, as well as building awards – and to contribute to costs of entry or to take a table at awards ceremonies.

- Extension of current commission(s) to further stages and phases.

- For client to accept invitation and attend as guest at suitable events, or send representative.

- Providing a glowing client reference to be used in a range of media – on data sheets, on website, in bidding documents, in monographs.

- Provision of more opportunities, long listings, short listings and / or commissions.

- Resolution of services, support and fees for post-completion periods.

- Collaboration on lessons learned or feedback arrangements.

- Retention of position and participation on frameworks.

- Introductions and recommendations to others as available.

And who knows where some of these options may lead in enhanced relationships, new contacts and connections, positive profiles, new opportunities for fee-earning commissions and rewarding workload.

As may be seen many of these ideas are win: win situations where previous difficulties, including dealing with additional fees, can be put to bed and matters can move forward. Some of these aspects can also heal stresses and strains within the team, as well as with the client / employer.

It probably was never only just about the money!

And back to monetary terms there are possible tax credits for research and development which may be general or aligned to particular projects.

15. conclusions

As we say on the back cover, asking for extra fees, efficiently and effectively for growing numbers of commissions is going to become important and necessary for the survival, prosperity and morale of many conventional and niche architectural and other professional practices in the property and construction sectors.

We hope that the diverse considerations on extra fees in this volume provide sufficient tips and tricks to deal with such matters in theory and practice, with confidence and clarity of purpose – with positive results.

And we should not forget the basic steps which were provided at the very start of this volume, with a variation in Appendix D just to reinforce the points.

Best wishes with it all.

"Cheers!"

For the full range of dashdot services and products, including consultancy services for Extra Fees, please visit www.dashdot.co.uk.

appendices

a. exercises – the McGivity conundrums.

Mrs McGivity at Rose Cottage

McGivity and McGivity
at Pott Chambers

McGivity Developments
at Whiteland House

McGivity Fashions:
No.1 on the High Street

Resiblitz

The Manor Park

McGivity Blooms

Big McG

McGivity Hotels and Leisure

b. typical appointment clauses

c. possible situations checklist

d. typical documents – when asking for additional fees.

e. basic steps – again.

f. references.

a. exercises – the McGivity conundrums

Welcome to the McGivity Conundrums.

These nine tests can be explored by individuals, or in teams, or across groups – to identify themes, undertake analysis, resolve recommendations, discuss in CPD sessions, etc. – or just read over and imagine the options.

There is a wide range of situations, timings and approaches in relation to dealing with possible extras and additional fees as may be seen from these conundrums.

And different people in different practices will have different interpretations depending on their confidence and circumstances.

It is possible to be objectively dispassionate and rational in dealing with hypothetical situations – as these exercises. It may be more difficult to be applied subjectively when personally and directly involved in real time, in real life situations.

There may also be immediate knee-jerk or gut reactions to situations and then there may be slower, considered thinking, diverse solutions and recommended routes – which can be tested through these conundrums.

It is possible for the proposed responses to these conundrums to be presented to an existing or nascent "NegMent" individual or group – see end of section 11.

Mrs McGivity at Rose Cottage

Granny McGivity is a charming, elderly widow and near neighbour who would like a kitchen extension with the money she has received from her deceased sister (early Covid plus underlying health problems). And you have agreed to be her architect.

At the start of the construction work she realises that she has more inheritance than she was expecting. She would like a new porch on the front door as well.

What is your approach to this extra work and possible additional fees?

McGivity and McGivity is one of the leading firms of sharp solicitors in a regional city. They specialise including in property and construction. They have appointed your practice to be the architect or design professional for the fitout of their new offices for a combined staff of 400 people – within shell and core base build which is under construction.

After obtaining layout signoffs, budget resolutions and landlord's approval you are informed that another legal practice of 200 people has been incorporated and accordingly they have taken another floor. Complications! Reviews!

Then a few weeks later that they may be taken over themselves. Suspension!

After a delay of four months this has blown over, however now they would like to include a gym and a healthy eating café. Then unexpectedly a pandemic has arrived, and they are considering all their options for working-from-home and technology upgrades.

They would still like to go out to competitive tender on the initial scheme – resolve the major and minor variations and negotiate with a suitable fit-out contractor.

What are your approaches to this extra work and possible additional fees?

McGivity Developments at Whiteland House

McGivity Developments are leading developers of commercial property for which you have an ongoing relationship as architect or designer – in this case for a £15m offices new build on an urban site. Initially it was anticipated that planning permission could be achieved in twelve months. For various reasons, including demise definitions, pandemic impacts and local elections it took twenty months.

What were your approaches to this prolongation?

Thereafter you were novated to a Design and Build contractor (at £16m contract sum) with the remainder of your original fee.

Initially the construction duration on site was to be twelve months.

For various reasons including partial site vacation, geotechnical issues, impact of pandemic, etc the practical completion was achieved in eighteen months.

What were your approaches to this prolongation?

McGivity Fashions: No.1 on the High Street

McGivity Fashions are up and coming, environmentally aware retailers with combinations of retail units, on-line shopping, warehouses and offices. They are notorious for being at the cutting edge and constantly changing their minds to stay there.

The owners are an interesting, family combination of creatives and accountants who are known to be demanding of the supply chain.

They would like a new reception, new meetings and board rooms with adjacent social spaces and catering support. Their overall budget expectation seems low at £2-4m.

What is your approach to their request for a FIXED fee for architectural or other professional services?

Resiblitz

M'givitydotkom, the marmalade to missiles conglomerate, have announced the building of factories to make one million per annum (!) prefabricated, low cost, starter housing units for UK and then worldwide. There are political considerations such as ten "regional" factories at £40m each or four "national" factories at £75m each. The steering group would like to know what differences these options might make to your architect or other professional fees. Any thoughts?

Also whether the first factory makes the components to build the following factories or should existing industrial premises be rented and repurposed to come on stream ASAP.

Any more thoughts on fee permutations? Also they are seeking bids from design consortia. Okay to provide or advise on some aggregated fees?

The Manor Park

Ms McGivity has received a recommendation for your services, from her grandmother Granny McGivity, to advise on some aspects of the layout of an eco-camping site she is setting up and managing in a royal park.

Initially it is only some thoughts on an access road and some trees next to power lines – which she anticipates would need a site visit and a day or so. But it is 500 miles away.

She may be related to some other McGivitys possibly involved in the law or fashion or development.

Any thoughts?

McGivity Blooms

McGivity Blooms had appointed you as designers for 100 organic flower and chocolate stalls at railway stations with a £25k shop fit for each.

Based on this £2.5m works budget you had quoted a fee of 5% or £125k paid as works proceed.

After a lot of effort the first prototype was completed. However the target number had been changed to forty units. After difficulties in securing suitable sites the business model was changed again with expectation of ten units at £40k each.

After completing four units the units and concept were sold on to others who had their own team; and McG Blooms moved into currency exchange retail units – with a new team.

How do you suggest the flower and chocolates stalls fee situation is resolved – or shall it be put down to experience?

Big McG

The design stage of the refurbishment of a local community centre (£5m construction budget) is underway, supported by the McGivity Philanthropic Fund. Site surveys have uncovered issues with asbestos, lead paint, cracked drains and mercury between floorboards from use in 1940s. £1million of extra funds have been found to deal with these complications.

What might be the reasoning for and against architects and other professionals recovering additional fees on these further elements and increased budget?

McGivity Hotels and Leisure

This one hundred and ten bedroom, three star hotel, next to a railway station has been designed, budgeted, signed off and submitted for town planning. Hooray!

However a number of internal client heads of departments and their advisors are now sending emails with requirements and asking for meetings including for front of house, housekeeping, branding, public relations, leisure and fitness, food and beverages, facilities management.

How is this going to be handled, including from resourcing and fee points of view? (It is noted that the hotel development managers seem to have moved on to their next enterprise opportunity!)

appendices

b. typical appointment clauses

Back to basics.

The following pages provide some typical or indicative terms and clauses related to additional fees that may be found in appointment documentation for "Consultants" including architects and other professionals.

Let's start with definitions and interpretations, or the vocabulary, which are used in the clauses and terms and conditions:

Basic Services means the services to be provided by the consultant under this agreement as set out in the Consultant's letter of offer / in Appendix XX.

Basic Fee means the amount payable by the Client to the Consultant for the Basic Services under this agreement as set out in the Consultant's letter of offer / in Appendix YY.

That will lead to:

Additional Services means any additional services over and above the Basic Services agreed between the Parties, notified to the Consultant after the date of this agreement or as may otherwise be required.

Additional Fee means the amount payable by the Client to the Consultant for the Additional Services under this Agreement.

So consequently in this instance:

Services means the Basic Services and the Additional Services.

Fees means Consultant's fees for the Services, including the Basic Fee and the Additional Fee.

These terms will then appear in clauses which are relevant to additional fees such as:

 # The Consultant shall provide the Services with the reasonable skill, care and diligence as may reasonably be expected of appropriately qualified and experienced consultants with appropriate skill and experience of providing services of a similar scope, type, nature, value and complexity to the Services.

So in this instance that applies as much to the Additional Services as to the Basic Services and similar skill, care and diligence should be applied.

Moving on to payments:

 # The Client shall pay the Basic Fee as full remuneration for the Basic Services and the Additional Fee as full remuneration for any Additional Services. The Fee is exclusive of VAT and any disbursements or expenses which shall be payable by the Client.

 # Payments to the Consultant shall be become due on submission of the Consultant's invoice to the Client (the "due date"). The final date of payment of any invoice shall be (14) days from the due date.

So in this case the same payment arrangements will apply to the Additional Fees as well as the Basic Fees.

And in the case of difficulties:

 # No later than five days after the payment becomes due, the Client shall notify the Consultant of the sum that the Client considers to have been due at the payment due date and the basis on which that sum is calculated.

There will probably also be clauses covering "pay less" arrangements – as counterclaims.

In relation to Variation or Extra or Additional Services:

 # The Consultant shall notify the Client as soon as reasonably practicable if it becomes apparent that Additional Services are required.

The Fee shall be adjusted and/or increased by a fair and reasonable amount if the performance of the Services is materially delayed or disrupted due to a change in the scope, size, complexity or duration of the Project, and/or if the Consultant is required to provide Additional Services.

Without limitation to the foregoing, if performance of the Services is delayed, disrupted or otherwise impacted in any way whatsoever by a Pandemic event, the Fee shall be increased by a fair and reasonable amount to reflect such delay, disruption or other impact.

Either Party may request a change to the scope or execution of the Services. The Consultant has no obligation to perform any varied or Additional Services unless the Parties have agreed any adjustments to the Basic or Additional Fees. However, failure to agree the Basic or Additional Fees prior to the Consultant performing varied or Additional Services shall not bar the Consultant from claiming an adjustment to the Basic or Additional Fees at a later date.

And there may be clauses which explain the reasons for entitlement to additional fees on the lines of the following.

[How many of the possible situations in Section 2 above align with these contractual avenues?]

 # If the (consultant / Architect / designer), for reasons beyond their control is involved in extra work or incurs extra expense, for which they will not otherwise be remunerated, they shall be entitled to additional fees calculated on a time basis unless otherwise agreed.

Reasons for such entitlement include, but shall not be limited to:

- *The scope of the Services or the Timetable or the period specified for any work stage is varied by the Client.*

- *The nature of the Project requires that substantial parts of the design cannot be completed or must be specified provisionally or approximately before construction commences.*

- *The (Consultant) being required to vary any item of work commenced or completed pursuant to the Agreement or to provide a new design after the Client has authorised the (Consultant) to develop an approved design.*

- *Delay or disruption by others.*

- *Prolongation of any building contract(s) related to the Project.*

- *the (Consultant) consenting to enter into a third-party agreement the form or beneficiary of which had not been agreed by the (Consultant) at the date of the Agreement.*

- *The cost of any work designed by the (Consultant) or the cost of special equipment is excluded from the Construction Cost.*

This clause shall not apply where the extra work and/or expense to which it refers is due to a breach of the Agreement by the (Consultant).

Should a dispute arise concerning Additional Fees there will be options:

 # Either Party may at any time refer a dispute or difference arising under this Agreement to adjudication. The Adjudication shall be conducted in accordance with TeCSA Adjudication Rules from time to time in force.

[The Technology and Construction Solicitor Association – other adjudication arrangements are available.]

And then there are the legal routes – including for Additional Fees:

 # This Agreement shall be governed by and construed in accordance with xxxx law and the xxxx courts shall have exclusive jurisdiction over any dispute or difference that may arise under or in connection with it.

The legal jurisdiction may be influenced by the locations of the project and of the client organisation. For UK consultants it will be worth considering carefully and consulting advisors if the jurisdiction is outside the UK.

NOTES:

appendices

c. possible situations checklist

The following pages provide a summary of the group headings and topic titles from Section 2 as a CHECKLIST.

2.1. SCOPE CHANGES

2.1.1 Increases in the Construction or Project Budget.

☐ Percentage based fee?
☐ Fixed or capped fee?
☐ Decrease in fee?
☐ Project budget?
☐ Construction budget?

2.1.2 More Units.

☐ More?
☐ or Less?
☐ Per Unit fees?
☐ Sliding Scales?
☐ Nominal?
☐ No Extra Fees at all?

2.1.3 Scope Enlargements.

☐ New requirements under a shell and core scheme?
☐ Expansion of external works?
☐ Public realm?
☐ Site or location opportunities – or restraints.
☐ Covered by indemnity insurance?

2.1.4 Inflation.

☐ Project inflation – Project growing or expanding?
☐ Financial inflation? Fixed budget: Less buying power?
☐ Extra work to resolve?
☐ How much extra work?

2.2. TIME CHANGES

2.2.1 Time Refinements.

Increases (or decreases) for:
- ☐ Project phasing?
- ☐ Changes of priorities?
- ☐ Revised sequencing?
- ☐ Sectional completions?
- ☐ Partial possessions?
- ☐ Pre-site and on site?
- ☐ Other?

2.2.2 Stop : Start

- ☐ Impact on the total workload?
- ☐ Tick-over contributions while stopped?
- ☐ Remobilisation on restart?
- ☐ Changes or impacts on the work to date – possibly as a result of the cause of the stoppage?

2.2.3 All Stages Taking Longer.

- ☐ Project has grown in size?
- ☐ Target dates over-ambitious?
- ☐ Workload the same – just longer periods?
- ☐ Increasing numbers of meetings, reviews, reports needed?

2.2.4 One Stage Taking Longer.

- ☐ Significant extra efforts to undertake – or not?
- ☐ Can such efforts be clearly identified, quantified and verified – or not?
- ☐ Acceleration or special efforts needed in later stages?

2.2.5 Acceleration.

- ☐ Acceleration needed to minimise critical delay?
- ☐ Overtime or special measures applied to achieve target dates or ameliorate delays?
- ☐ In isolation?
- ☐ Multiple times?
- ☐ Recoverable as extra fees?

2.3. PEOPLE AND ORGANISATIONAL CHANGES

2.3.1 More People and Organisations.

☐ Increase in the number and involvements of stakeholders?

☐ Increase in the number and involvements of team participants?

☐ Extra work?

☐ How much extra work?

2.3.2 Changes of People and Organisations.

☐ Are there departures of some parties?

☐ Selections, arrivals and inductions of new parties?

☐ Does this cause knock-on time delay consequences?

☐ Does this generate extra work?

☐ How much extra work?

2.3.3 More Interaction.

Interaction becoming more or too much interaction? Such as for:

☐ Town planning mutual solutions, extended statutory difficulties, utility negotiations.

Or dealing with stakeholders such as:

☐ neighbours, special interest groups, prospective tenants or occupiers, etc.

☐ Above foreseeable involvements at time of bidding?

☐ How much extra interaction?

2.3.4 Design Team Leadership and Management

☐ Size and membership of the design team increased?

☐ More Team management than expected?

☐ Over a longer period of time?

☐ A case for additional fees – or not?

2.3.5 Changes in Procurement Arrangements

☐ Single stage or two stage?

☐ Two stage formats / approaches?

☐ Single stage negotiation – to – multiple tenderers?

2.3.6 Changes to Contract Arrangements

☐ Traditional or Design and Build or Construction Management?

☐ Or some Client Orders?

☐ NEC Forms?

2.4. DESIGN CHANGES

2.4.1 Design Information from Others.

- ☐ Multiple issues or complex aspects?
- ☐ Design information compiled from consultants, specialist designers?
- ☐ Samples, assemblies, testing, prototypes?
- ☐ Over and above expected editions, iterations and durations?
- ☐ How much extra work?

2.4.2 Analysis and Comments.

- ☐ For tenants' or occupiers' proposals for landlords' approvals?
- ☐ Not included in the appointment documentation?
- ☐ Or excessive?
- ☐ Similarly when acting on behalf of tenants and occupiers?

2.4.3 Achieving Alignments.

- ☐ Adjustment of information to fit the Contractors Proposals in design and Build.
- ☐ New purchaser / owner modifications to established scheme.
- ☐ Excessive extra work?
- ☐ Reimbursable?

2.4.4 Revised Criteria.

- ☐ New or revised criteria or brief requirements?
- ☐ To be assessed and implemented e.g. building standards, regulation?
- ☐ Also changes to sector, environmental, marketplace standards.
- ☐ Due to pandemics?
- ☐ And others?

2.4.5 Design Iteration.

- ☐ Some creative iteration expected within design stages.
- ☐ But iteration can be due to problem solving
- ☐ Or repetitive or "out-of-stage".
- ☐ A case for additional fees – or not?

2.5. ADMINISTRATIVE CHANGES

2.5.1 More Visits.

- ☐ Number of visits in excess of the total in appointment documents?
- ☐ More types of visits?
- ☐ More than might be reasonably expected?
- ☐ Including post practical completion visits?

2.5.2 Revising Information.

- ☐ Excessive revisions and reissues of information?
- ☐ For external reasons, which may justify additional fees?
- ☐ Or internal design development, corrections, additions?
- ☐ During Stages 4, 5 and 6.

2.5.3 Additional Exercises.

- ☐ More additional exercises than agreed or expected?
- ☐ Further value engineering, risk assessments, principals' meetings, retendering or cost reduction?
- ☐ Independently or integrated with others?
- ☐ Implementing through revised design and other project information

2.5.4 Additional Expenses.

- ☐ For travel and accommodation; deliveries and couriers;
- ☐ Special printing; postage and delivery;
- ☐ Photography and video;
- ☐ Provision of space and facilities for group working in short term or over longer periods.

2.5.5 Change Assessments.

- ☐ Change control procedures, over and above the norm?
- ☐ More frequent and extensive than envisaged?
- ☐ Consuming resources and expertise?
- ☐ Subsequent revision and reissue of information?

2.6. MISCELLANEOUS TOPICS

2.6.1 Payments on Behalf of Client

- ☐ Placing orders and making payments on behalf of the client?
- ☐ Pre-agreed handling charges.
- ☐ E.g. model making, surveys and investigations, purchasing samples,
- ☐ Travel disbursements for shared trips,
- ☐ Subcontract designers or for other specialist services.

2.6.2 Pre-agreed Bonuses.

- ☐ A pre-agreed bonus arrangement in place?
- ☐ For when the target has been achieved,
- ☐ E.g. planning permissions, scope or timing, sign-offs – as pre-agreed?
- ☐ Separate invoice may be submitted?

2.6.3 Promotional Needs.

- ☐ Special promotional material or activity.
- ☐ Official launches or openings, enhanced handover documentation, submissions for prizes and awards, project monographs, etc.
- ☐ Professional beneficial non-cash side effects?
- ☐ Or extra fees? Or shared?

2.6.4 Combined, Joint or Multiple Situations.

- ☐ Collaborative, integrated services?
- ☐ "Not part of the appointment"?
- ☐ Extra fees?

2.6.5 Additional Premiums.

- ☐ Professional Indemnity Insurance
- ☐ Above standard levels, durations,
- ☐ Dependent on the marketplace
- ☐ To be paid or shared?

2.6.6 The Unexpected.

- ☐ Unexpected surprises – in theory and in practice?
- ☐ Extra work that can be quantified and recovered as additional fees?
- ☐ Or working round? Such as pandemics, strikes and industrial action, etc?

2.7. SERVICE CHANGES

2.7.1 Duties.

- ☐ Optional duties included with the core duties and the base fee.
- ☐ Additional fees are likely to be charged and recovered.
- ☐ What are the core duties – and optional duties (unlikely and excluded).
- ☐ E.g. modern post occupancy support and advice,

2.7.2 Assessment of Claims.

- ☐ Claims by others?
- ☐ Or advising client on claims from other design team members.
- ☐ Are these additional services?

2.7.3 Excessive Complications.

- ☐ Disruptive, distracting and consuming resources.
- ☐ May be recoverable if one is not the source?
- ☐ Additional people needed?
- ☐ Acceleration measures?

2.7.4 Additional Efforts.

- ☐ Additional efforts needed?
- ☐ Site circumstances, contractual difficulties, etc?
- ☐ Recoverable or simply "best endeavours"?
- ☐ Above the norm? Or "whatever it takes"?

2.7.5 Contingencies in Budgets.

- ☐ Known contingencies in project budgets?
- ☐ Applicable to your fees?
- ☐ What provisions in your fee calculations to deal with "extra work" etc.?

appendices

d. typical documents – when asking for extra fees.

Suitable typical, internal or useful project documents, with locations or contacts as sources can be referenced or listed here, or at the end of this volume.

These can be:

- Copies of sections of real appointment documentation pertinent to extra fees – see appendix b. for examples.

- Examples of real minutes, notes, emails, confirmation of instructions, covering notifications of possible additional activities or services that may or will incur additional costs – that in due course will be converted into additional fees to be recovered.

- Examples of applications for additional fees including schedules of attachments, as evidence – see section 14 for guidance.

- Exchanges of correspondence on resolving additional fees.

- Notes on strategies and approaches to negotiations for additional fees.

Anonymise if appropriate.

appendices

e. CHECKLIST – basic steps – again.

Hello again! Let's remind ourselves again of the basic steps when it comes to extras and extra fees.

Step One: Amongst other things, when involved with opportunities and enquiries with proposals and bids, please identify the extras or changes which are likely to arise during the project and to the services – from checklists and experience, by stages and overall.

Step Two: Check that suitable provisions to deal with such extras and changes are within the orders, contracts or appointment documents – and the provisions are clear, comprehensive, fair and quantifiable – as standard terms and conditions.

Step Three: However if extras and changes are likely or inevitable but costs will be difficult to recover, please make suitable contingency provisions in the base fee or tender. Or provide exclusion clauses or limits and seek agreement.

STEP FOUR: Please undertake Steps 1, 2 and 3 **before** entering into or signing any agreement or starting work! Or cap the scope, values or durations of initial or next stage involvements – in writing.

Step Five: When appointed, communicate the arrangements and boundaries concerning extras and changes to key project staff.

Step Six: As the possible extras or changes arise, verify how they are covered within the agreements, and apply the arrangements.

Step Seven: If significant resources and cost will be incurred in assessing or implementing each extra or change, obtain understandings on payments – in detail or in principle – in advance. Or decline. Or dip into the contingency provisions. Or sacrifice some margin / profit.

Step Eight: Identify and regularly maintain the procedures, lines of communication and contacts for addressing and recovering additional costs.

Step Nine: Monitor patterns of extras and changes, with their fee recovery or compensation or impacts on contingency provisions or bottom line.

Step Ten: Please make sure the base services, outputs, products and deliverables are fully, promptly and properly provided, so there are no excuses, set offs or counterclaims that may affect the entitlements arising from the extras and changes.

If these basic steps are not in place or are not working as you wish, then please return selectively to the contents and checklists within this volume.

f. references.

"Getting Paid. An Architect's guide to fee recovery claims."

By Nicholas J. Carnell and Stephen Yakeley
Published by RIBA Enterprises 2003.

"Architect's Handbook of Practice Management" 9th Edition

By Nigel Ostime.
Published by RIBA Publishing 2013

"Good Practice Guide – Fees"

By Peter Farrell and Stephen Brookhouse.
Published by RIBA Publishing 2021.

"This guide is written for architects who are either sole practioners or work in micro and small practices and whose clients are, in the main, domestic end users."

Also includes some interesting Cautionary Tales and Good Practice Examples.

"Standard Professional Services Contract 2020 Architectural Services"

By Royal Institute of British Architects.

This volume is from a range of available standards which contain relevant terms and conditions, similar to those in Appendix B Typical Appointment Clauses within. Other appointment documents are available.

"Thinking Fast and Slow!'

By Daniel Kahneman
Published by Penguin Books 2012

This book is included because there are often knee-jerk reactions when mentioning extra fees by all sides which might be overcome with some more considered thinking.

"Time Matters" (see pages 25 and 74)

By Tom Taylor
Published by dashdot publications 2017

"Leadership in Action" (see page 47)

by Tom Taylor
Published by dashdot publications 2011, including MAG Factor – management, administration and guidance.

"An Introduction to and a Study Guide for Collaboration – for contractor contributions to design team activities" (see page 77)

By Tom Taylor
Published by dashdot publications 2015

"An Introduction to the Ever Expanding Design Team"

By Tom Taylor
Published by dashdot publications 2013

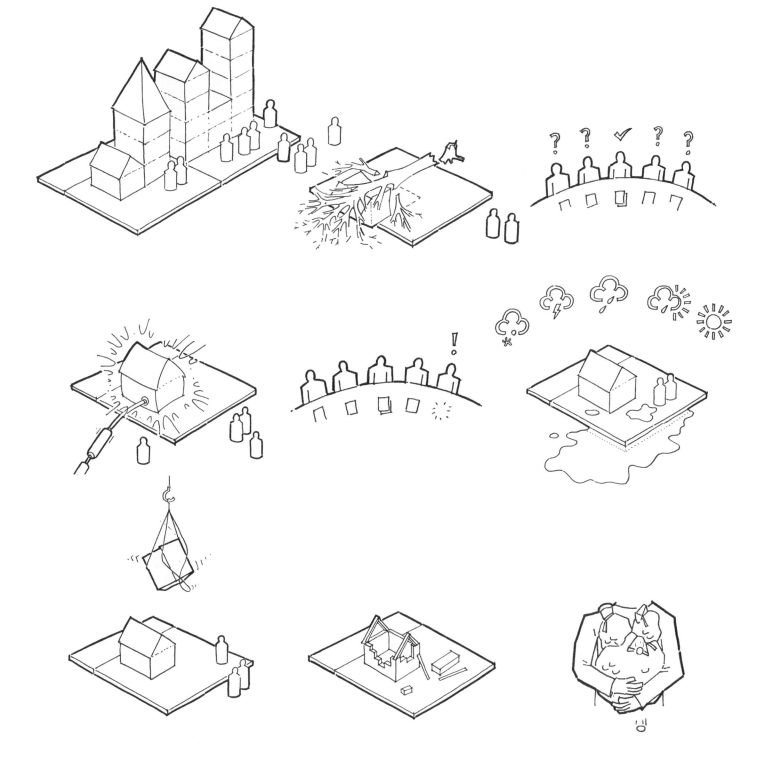